Social Studies on the Internet

THIRD EDITION

Michael J. Berson
University of South Florida

Bárbara C. Cruz
University of South Florida

James A. Duplass
University of South Florida

J. Howard Johnston
University of South Florida

PEARSON

Merrill
Prentice Hall

Upper Saddle River, New Jersey
Columbus, Ohio

Library of Congress Cataloging-in-Publication Data
Social studies on the Internet/ Michael J. Berson . . . [et al.].—3rd ed.
  p. cm.
  ISBN 0-13-238319-5 (paperback)
   1. Social sciences—Study and teaching—United States—Computer network resources.
   2. Internet in education—United States. I. Berson, Michael J.
LB1584.7.S63 2007
300'.2854678—dc22

2006043244

Vice President and Executive Publisher: Jeffery W. Johnston
Senior Acquisitions Editor: Allyson P. Sharp
Senior Editorial Assistant: Kathleen S. Burk
Production Editor: Alexandrina Benedicto Wolf
Production Coordination: GGS Book Services
Design Coordinator: Diane C. Lorenzo
Cover Designer: Bryan Huber
Cover Image: Corbis
Production Manager: Pamela D. Bennett
Director of Marketing: David Gesell
Senior Marketing Manager: Darcy Betts Prybella
Marketing Coordinator: Brian Mounts

This book was set in Minion by GGS Book Services. It was printed and bound by R.R.
Donnelley & Sons Company. The cover was printed by R.R. Donnelley & Sons Company.

Pearson Education Ltd.   Pearson Education Australia Pty. Limited
Pearson Education Singapore Pte. Ltd.   Pearson Education North Asia Ltd.
Pearson Education Canada, Ltd.   Pearson Educación de Mexico, S.A. de C.V.
Pearson Education—Japan   Pearson Education Malaysia Pte. Ltd.

10 9 8 7 6 5 4 3 2
ISBN 0-13-238319-5

For our families:

Ilene, Elisa, and Marc

Kevin, Cristina, and Amanda

Anne, Chris, Tina, Lizzie, Carly, Ellie, and Manny

Lucinda, Christopher, Lisa, Kristin, and Dan

Teacher Preparation Classroom

TEACHER PREP

MERRILL
PRENTICE HALL

See a demo at
www.prenhall.com/teacherprep/demo

Your Class. Their Careers. Our Future. Will Your Students Be Prepared?

We invite you to explore our new, innovative and engaging website and all that it has to offer you, your course, and tomorrow's educators! Organized around the major courses pre-service teachers take, the Teacher Preparation site provides media, student/teacher artifacts, strategies, research articles, and other resources to equip your students with the quality tools needed to excel in their courses and prepare them for their first classroom.

This ultimate on-line education resource is available at no cost, when packaged with a Merrill text, and will provide you and your students access to:

Online Video Library. More than 150 video clips—each tied to a course topic and framed by learning goals and Praxis-type questions—capture real teachers and students working in real classrooms, as well as in-depth interviews with both students and educators.

Student and Teacher Artifacts. More than 200 student and teacher classroom artifacts—each tied to a course topic and framed by learning goals and application questions—provide a wealth of materials and experiences to help make your study to become a professional teacher more concrete and hands-on.

Research Articles. Over 500 articles from ASCD's renowned journal *Educational Leadership*. The site also includes *Research Navigator*, a searchable database of additional educational journals.

Teaching Strategies. Over 500 strategies and lesson plans for you to use when you become a practicing professional.

Licensure and Career Tools. Resources devoted to helping you pass your licensure exam; learn standards, law, and public policies; plan a teaching portfolio; and succeed in your first year of teaching.

How to ORDER *Teacher Prep* for you and your students:

For students to receive a *Teacher Prep* Access Code with this text, instructors **must** provide a special value pack ISBN number on their textbook order form. To receive this special ISBN, please email **Merrill.marketing@pearsoned.com** and provide the following information:

- Name and Affiliation
- Author/Title/Edition of Merrill text

Upon ordering *Teacher Prep* for their students, instructors will be given a lifetime *Teacher Prep* Access Code.

Preface

[This technology] is destined to revolutionize our educational system and . . . in a few years it will supplant largely, if not entirely, the use of textbooks.

Thomas Edison, 1922, statement on the invention of film

Claims of the importance of new technologies by the inventors are not limited to current cultural advancements. Society's pundits have customarily proclaimed that advances in technology will reshape the face of the human experience. Historians note that the "Gutenberg Revolution" reshaped the knowledge base, access to information, and learning process of Western civilization. Perhaps not as apparent, subsequent advances such as the chalkboard, ballpoint pen, mass production of paper, mimeograph machine, public library, overhead projector, radio, and television have changed how we learn. The significance of the Internet, as a societal and learning force, might be surpassed only by the invention of written language. Marshall McLuhan's declaration—that the problem today isn't that we don't have the answers, but that we don't have the questions—prophesied the new world of information created by the Internet.

Social Studies on the Internet is an annotated collection of websites designed for current and future teachers of social studies at the elementary, middle, and high school levels. It is a new doorway to the best practices, content, and original ideas that are essential to the success of social studies teachers. Mastery of the Internet and its resources can greatly enhance the quality of the learning experience in social studies classrooms.

In this third edition:

- Every website has been checked, updated, or replaced.
- New websites have been added to reflect the tremendous growth and developments of the Internet.

Chapter 1 has been expanded to include GEM, the redeveloped ERIC, and other multipurpose websites. It now includes multidiscipline websites and introduces Internet terminology, various ways to use Internet resources, and sites that provide tutorials for less experienced users.

Chapter 2 deals with Internet safety, legal and ethical issues regarding use of material, and integrating the Internet into social studies instruction.

Chapters 3 through 10 contain a wide range of invaluable social studies resources for teachers at every level as they begin to use the Internet for their professional development, in their classroom learning experiences, and to change the way they teach. The websites are organized based on content topics so they are easily accessible as teachers prepare unit and lesson plans.

Chapters 11 and 12 offer a number of resources ranging from planning and setting goals to accommodating diverse student populations. Chapter 13 provides resources to help teachers grow professionally and effectively respond to classroom management challenges.

SELECTION OF SITES

In selecting the various websites, four criteria were used.

1. *Comprehensiveness.* We selected websites that offer the most comprehensive information and resources on important social studies topics.

2. *Durability.* It takes time, effort, and creativity to integrate the Internet into unit and lesson plans, and teachers need some reasonable assurance that their efforts will be useful in the future. Sponsoring organizations of national or regional reputation that support websites will more likely provide long-term stability and permanence, encouraging teachers to prepare lessons that integrate technology.

3. *Currency and Renewability.* We selected websites that have a history of improvements and innovations to make the sites more usable, accurate, and up-to-date.

4. *Credibility.* Content on the Internet is fluid and can be inaccurate. As in any medium, the source of the information is a major consideration in evaluating its accuracy. The Internet has made it possible for content to be published in such an inexpensive manner that availability is no longer an adequate screening device. The volume of information in relation to the areas of expertise of reviewers has made it impossible for individuals to validate content. Therefore, we emphasized sites with reputable, service-oriented patrons who are affiliated with well-respected organizations.

ORGANIZATION OF THE BOOK

In organizing the social studies content chapters (Chapters 3 through 10), we have identified gateway sites, specialized sites, the kinds of information provided, and connections to NCSS themes. These identifiers will help you determine the suitability of each site for your specific educational goals.

Sites

■ *Gateway websites* typically offer the most comprehensive access to information, multiple links to related websites, and/or multiple applications (such as information, lessons, simulations, and virtual field trips). These gateway websites appear first in each chapter or section of a chapter. Chapter 6's National Geographic website, **http://www.nationalgeographic.com,** is an example.

■ *Specialized websites* are typically focused on a specific topic, but may also be comprehensive. Although less inclusive, specialized websites include more focused collections of information or applications. The Betsy Ross home page at **http://www.ushistory.org/betsy** is one example of an elementary school-level site that is comprehensive, but on a limited topic. This website is a link within a more comprehensive topic, Philadelphia Area Historical Sites, **http://www.ushistory.org**, sponsored by the Independence Hall Association. Because it is limited to the American Revolutionary period, the Philadelphia Area Historical Sites website would more likely appear as a specialized website. These specialized websites follow the gateway websites in each chapter or section.

Application Icons

Each website in Chapters 3 through 10 will have one or more of these icons to indicate the kind of information that can be found in the website.

Icon	Title	Type of Information
	Asking Experts	An e-mail opportunity to communicate with experts
	Databases	A compilation of websites or a searchable database from which information may be selected and gleaned
	E-Mail Pals	An e-mail opportunity to communicate with other students
	Elementary Emphasis	Resources that may be particularly appropriate for elementary social studies instruction
	Lesson Plans	Lessons developed by practitioners or curriculum writers
	Primary Sources	Original documents that can be downloaded and used in instruction
	Simulations	Active learning experiences
	Technical Assistance	Resources to improve learning
	Virtual Field Trips	Full-motion video or frames of a location
	Online Projects	Continuous, real-time projects

NCSS Themes

A quick reference after each site includes the National Council for the Social Studies (NCSS) themes to assist readers in curriculum or lesson planning.

The 10 NCSS themes have been adopted nationally as the core of social studies instruction:

I	Culture
II	Time, Continuity, and Change
III	People, Places, and Environments
IV	Individual Development and Identity
V	Individuals, Groups, and Institutions
VI	Power, Authority, and Governance
VII	Production, Distribution, and Consumption
VIII	Science, Technology, and Society
IX	Global Connections
X	Civic Ideals and Practices

A full explanation of the themes appears on the NCSS website, **http://www.ncss.org/standards.** One or more of these Roman numerals following the description indicates that the website provides excellent instructional support instruction to achieve the indicated standard(s).

We believe these sites are valuable to social studies teachers as we strive to improve the quality of social studies education for the next generation of citizens in our country and the world.

Michael J. Berson
Bárbara C. Cruz
James A. Duplass
J. Howard Johnston

About the Authors

Michael J. Berson is Professor of Social Science Education at the University of South Florida (USF). He has received the USF Outstanding Undergraduate Teaching Award and has been honored with the National Council for the Social Studies (NCSS) President's Award for his exceptional contribution to the field. His courses have been recognized for integrating emerging technologies into instruction and modeling dynamic and fluid pedagogy. He cofounded the American Educational Research Association Special Interest Group Research in Global Child Advocacy; is a member of the Social Science Education Consortium, an international group of recognized scholars in social studies; and was Chair of the College and University Faculty Assembly of NCSS, and Vice President of the Society for Information Technology and Teacher Education. He is a consultant on the integration of technology into education and has participated in the National Technology Leadership Summit. He has extensively published books, chapters, and journal articles and presents worldwide. He conducts research on global child advocacy and technology in social studies education.

Bárbara C. Cruz is Professor of Social Science Education at the University of South Florida. Her research interests include global and multicultural perspectives in education, innovative teacher preparation practices, and active learning strategies. She is a frequent guest speaker on educational issues concerning minorities. Her work has been published in *Social Education, Multicultural Perspectives, Social Studies and the Young Learner,* and *OAH Magazine of History.* She is the author of several Latino and African American biographies and young adult books on educational issues such as school dress codes, single-sex education, and school violence. Her books *Multiethnic Teens and Cultural Identity* and *Alvin Ailey: Celebrating African-American Culture Through Dance* both won the Carter G. Woodson Book Award, granted annually for the most distinguished social science books appropriate for young readers that depict ethnicity in the United States.

James A. Duplass is Professor of Social Science Education at the University of South Florida. His research focus is on philosophical foundations of social sciences education, technology integration, methods of instruction, and competing conceptions of curriculum for social sciences education. He has received more than one million dollars in technology grants. He has published articles on values education, curriculum design, instructional methods, thinking skills, and administrative practices in higher education in *Middle Level Learning,* the *International Journal of Social Education, Trends and Issues, Technology Tools in the Social Sciences Curriculum,* the *Social Studies Review,* the *Social Studies, Computers and Education, College and University, Lyra Journal of Poetry and Fiction, Liberal Education,* and *Religious Education.* He is the past editor of *Trends and Issues.* Other publications include

Middle and High School Teaching: Methods, Standards and Best Practices (Houghton Mifflin, 2006); *Teaching Elementary Social Studies: What Every Teacher Should Know!* (Houghton Mifflin, 2004); *Elementary Education on the Internet* (Prentice Hall, 2006); and *Crescent City Short Stories,* a collection of southern ethnology themes.

J. Howard Johnston is Professor of Secondary Education at the University of South Florida. He has authored more than 100 works on middle-level education and has presented more than 1,500 invited papers, lectures, and keynote addresses throughout the United States, Canada, and in various countries in Europe, South America, Asia, and the Caribbean. In addition to nine books, he has published in the *NASSP Bulletin, Middle School Journal, Phi Delta Kappan, School Administrator, Schools in the Middle,* and *School Boards Journal,* among others. He is the recipient of the National Association of Secondary School Principals' Distinguished Service Award; the National Middle School Association's John Lounsbury Award for lifetime service; and the Gruhn-Long-Melton Award for lifetime service to middle-level education. He served on the Board of Trustees of the National Middle School Association and the Council on Middle Level Education for the National Association of Secondary School Principals, and is a lead team consultant for the Principals' Partnership, sponsored by Union Pacific.

Brief Contents

Contents

Note: Every effort has been made to provide accurate and current Internet information in this book. However, the Internet and information posted on it are constantly changing, so it is inevitable that some of the Internet addresses listed in this textbook will change.

Internet Basics and Multidiscipline Sites

The purpose of this chapter is to review some Internet basics and terminology and to provide you with a number of major sites that have been developed for teachers that cut across the social studies disciplines.

INTERNET BASICS

The Internet is a global arrangement of networks made up of millions of individual computers. Its primary capability is known as the **World Wide Web** ("WWW" or "the web"). The U.S. Department of Defense laid the foundation of the Internet more than 30 years ago with ARPANET. In 1993, there were approximately 130 websites; now there are millions. For a history of the Internet go to http://www.isoc.org/internet/history/brief.shtml and Hobbes' Internet Timeline http://www.zakon.org/robert/internet/timeline/.

To organize the information on the World Wide Web, **uniform resource locators** (URLs) were created to provide site addresses. As an example, the National Council for Social Studies is http://www.socialstudies.org (see Example 1-1). By having an address, you can use a browser (Internet Explorer, Netscape, etc.) to move from one website to another. The initial online view, such as http://www.socialstudies.org, is referred to as a **home page** or **web page**.

If you know the address of a site that you want to visit, you can type the address in the Location box at the top part of the browser (see Example 1-1) and press the Enter key. The software will process the request and take you to the website. You must type the address exactly, or you will receive a message indicating that the location cannot be found. Addresses can change from time to time, but often the old address will point you to the new address. In this book, we provide both the name of the sponsor and the URL. Should you go to one of the websites cited in this text and it does not produce the expected result, type in the name of the sponsor, such as "NCSS," and you will still be able to reach the website. In addition, you should be aware that names can be misleading. For example, Whitehouse.gov is the site for the White House of the United States of America; Whitehouse.com is not a government website or affiliated with the White House.

Example 1-1   A Home Page

Reprinted with permission of the National Council for the Social Studies.

Table 1-1   Domains

Domain	Type	Example	Source
.com	Commercial organization	dell.com	Dell Computer Corporation
.edu	Educational institution	usf.edu	University of South Florida
.gov	Government organization	lcweb.loc.gov	Library of Congress
.int	International organization	nato.int	NATO
.mil	Military site	monmouth.army.mil	Ft. Monmouth Army site
.net	Network organization	promo.net/drnet	Ask Dr. Internet
.org	Professional organization	NCSS.org	National Council for the Social Studies
.uk	Country	aaranet.co.uk	Aaranet is a network service in the United Kingdom

INTERNET ORGANIZATION ADDRESSES

Most people are familiar with the first part of the Internet address, which appears before the colon. This identifies the type of resource or method of access. For example, **http** stands for a hypertext document or directory. Less familiar but valid sources include **gopher, ftp, news, telnet, WAIS,** and **file.**

The second part of the address is usually the address of the computer where the data or service is located—typically, the home page. Additional parts may specify the name of a file, the port, or the text to search for in a database. The National Council for the Social Studies uses "social studies" to identify the home page in Example 1-1.

Domains classify broad types of providers based on their mission and are typically indicated by two or three letters. NCSS is an "org," for organization. Table 1-1 is a list of common domains.

BROWSERS AND SEARCH ENGINES

When you enter the web, the first page you see is the **browser** page. In this case it is Microsoft's Explorer (see the top line in Example 1-2). The organization displayed is the University of South Florida's public access page providing a WebQuest lesson in social studies to be used by middle and high school teachers. You may want to use some of these WebQuest lessons when you teach!

If you do not know the address of a website, the tool you can use to find information is a **search engine.** Example 1-2 includes two potential search engines: **Google's toolbar** is on the fourth line, where you would type into the **search box**

Example 1-2   Browsers and Search Engines

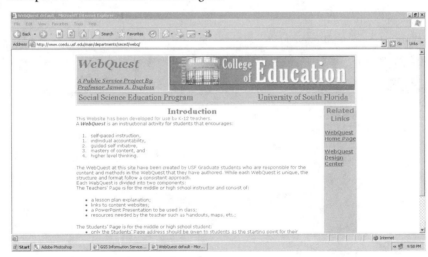

Permission granted by USF Social Studies Education.

the item you want to find ("American history lesson plans"). The **spyglass** icon on the third line can be used to access the **Microsoft Explorer** search engine. Other well-known search engines that are offered through **Netscape, About.com, Excite, Lycos,** and **Yahoo** also work in conjunction with browsers. If you want to add an additional search engine to your browser, enter one of the engine's names in your browser's search box and navigate to the download page. As an example, Google's toolbar can be downloaded from http://www.google.com/downloads/.

SEARCHING THE INTERNET

If you do not know a site's address but have a name like George Washington, NCSS, or National Council for the Social Studies, you can enter that information in the search box of the search engine, and it will return a new image listing possible sites that match the words you typed. No two search engines give the same results because they have different protocols for harvesting website locations. These listings of possible sites (see "George Washington" in Example 1-3) are known as **hits.** You can use search engines to search for various topics. You simply type in a word or phrase like "Ben Franklin," "De La Salle High School," "social studies lesson plans," or "Renaissance." Once the search engine provides the list of hits, you can click on any one of the items, and the search engine will take you to the website.

You can efficiently search the Internet by paying attention to a few simple rules. If you type "George Washington" (the quotes will give you only items with both George and Washington, rather than all Georges or all Washingtons) into the

Example 1-3   Search Engine Hits

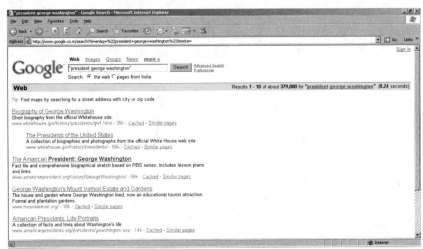

Google search box you will get more than 29 million hits because Google will list all sites mentioning both George *and* Washington. If you insert "President George Washington" you get more than 250,000. If you type "President George Washington" *and* "Mount Vernon," you produce 15,000 hits. The word *and* is an "operator." The most common and useful **operators** for searching are **AND, OR,** and **NOT**. Combined with " " to bracket terms and names, can greatly enhance your productivity in harvesting social studies materials and lesson plans for your classes.

TROUBLESHOOTING

You may find that a given website's address has been changed. Often, you will automatically be transferred to the new site. If this does not occur, you may try deleting any words or letters after the extension (e.g., the ".com" or ".edu"). Another strategy is to type in the name of the site in quotation marks in a search engine.

WEBSITE ORGANIZATION

There are four basic types of website organization:

1. A page of information, like the NCSS home page in Example 1-1, that you can scroll through to locate the exact information you are seeking.
2. A home page with internal links to pages within the website that are authored and controlled by the organization. Example 1-2 includes webquests authored by USF graduate students in social studies education and information on how to construct webquests.
3. A home page with internal links to pages within the website that are authored and controlled by the organization *and* with external links to other websites that are authored and controlled by other organizations. In some cases, one cannot tell which links are internal and which are external because they are not grouped separately. However, by the address of the new page you are sent to, you will know you have left the original URL (see Example 1-4).
4. A home page with only external links to other websites that are controlled and authored by other organizations. This would include results from your search engine (see Example 1-3). However, it would also include many sites from this book, like the World Wide Virtual Library: U.S. History http://vlib.iue.it/history/USA/.

NAVIGATION

One of the great assets of the Internet is the ease of navigation that is allowed with **clickable links.** Example 1-1 has multiple links, which appear as your mouse pointer passes over the seven headings at the top of the NCSS page. In Example 1-2, by clicking on "social studies" (not shown in image) at the bottom of the page, you can select "history" and then select from almost 25 webquests in Microsoft Word document form and with clickable links and web pages.

BOOKMARKS AND FAVORITES

Keeping track of your websites with your **Bookmark** or **Favorites** tool can mean significant savings for you in terms of time and keyboarding strokes. When you find a useful website, click on Bookmark at the top of the screen and add the site to your collection. As you harvest more and more valuable sites, you can then group your bookmarks into meaningful folders such as U.S. history, geography, and current events.

LEARNING MORE ABOUT THE INTERNET

If you would like to learn more about the Internet, Microsoft has a page for elementary and middle and high school teachers at http://office.microsoft.com/en-us/FX011387241033.aspx. At Webteacher, there is a tutorial on the Internet designed with teachers in mind (http://www.webteacher.org/windows.html).

Ultimately the best way to learn about the Internet is to explore. The subsequent chapters offer a wide range of social studies and education-related websites that provide points of departure into World Wide Web resources that will make a difference in the classroom experience of your students.

MULTIDISCIPLINE WEBSITES

The following are a number of multidiscipline and multipurpose websites that should be used by social studies teachers. Many include Internet lesson plans as well as various types of materials that can be infused into your lesson plans (see Chapter 12).

Example 1-4   Gateway to Educational Materials (GEM)

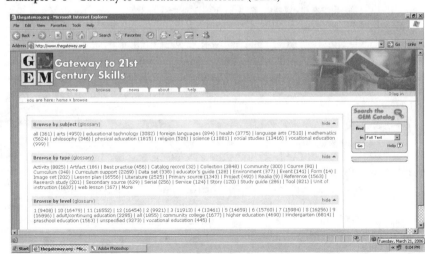

Gateway to Educational Materials (GEM)

This is a new service of the federal government developed for teachers by compiling various kinds of teaching resources in one location for easy access. It draws materials from public as well as commercial resources. You can search for a specific topic, like "Lincoln AND assassination," or you can navigate through links to narrow your search. In the image in Example 1-4, you can see that there are more than 13,000 social studies materials. If you click on "social studies," you will get a list of all the resources. While not shown as on image, from the list of social studies resources that are displayed you can select by subject area such as history or geography, grade level, topics like "Civil War," and so on. You can then select a lesson plan, materials, and so on. Once you are transferred to the link you clicked on, the address displayed in the Location box of the browser will indicate if it is an internal or external link. This distinction is important to social studies educators because decisions about the accuracy and credibility of information are in part dependent on its source.

ERIC (Educational Resources Information Center)

With more than 1 million documents, **ERIC** is the academic index used by most educators to locate current research on education topics. It has a degree of credibility that is not true of the Internet in general because most entries are reprinted from academic journals, conference presentations, and national reports. Many of ERIC's documents are **"full-text"** documents, which means the entire document can be retrieved online as a **PDF** (portable document format) file. The goal is to eventually have all documents available as full-text, online PDF files. In the past, teachers were forced to spend endless hours in the library and at a microfilm machine to find current and classic ideas on how to teach in new ways; now we have the Internet.

Go to http://www.eric.ed.gov (a page like Example 1-5 will be displayed) and select "Advanced Search." You will see that, when searching for documents based on a title, author, or keyword, you can request to view only those documents that are already available as full-text documents. Keep in mind that many of the best articles are not yet available online.

What Works Clearinghouse

A new initiative being implemented as a result of the No Child Left Behind legislation is the **What Works Clearinghouse** (WWC) at http://www.whatworks.ed.gov (see Example 1-6). This clearinghouse was established by the U.S. Department of Education's Institute of Education Sciences to provide educators, policymakers, and the public with a central source of scientific evidence of what works in education. Like ERIC, it houses publications about education; however, a major difference is that it limits its publications to reviews of scientific evidence of the effectiveness of replicable educational interventions (e.g., programs, practices, products, or policies) that promise to improve student outcomes.

Example 1-5   ERIC Advanced Search

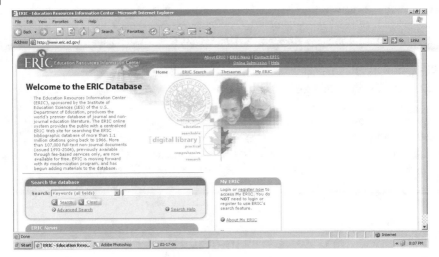

Example 1-6   What Works Clearinghouse

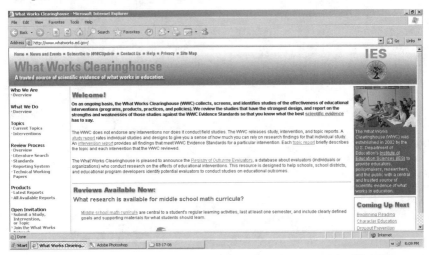

Anneberg/CPB's Learner.org

http://www.learner.org/index.html

This website offers online videos of teachers using best practices in classrooms with real students. You can select the discipline, subject, and grade level.

Core Knowledge

http://www.coreknowledge.org/CK/index.htm

> This site has extensive lesson plans for all grade levels in all the subject fields.

Teachervision

http://www.teachervision.fen.com/

> This site has multiple resources, including lesson plans, rubrics, and other materials.

National Endowment for the Humanities

http://edsitement.neh.gov

> The NEH maintains the Edsitement website with assets for all the humanities.

Discovery School

http://school.discovery.com/lessonplans

> This site allows you to select materials by subject field and grade level.

Lesson Plans Page

http://www.lessonplanspage.com/index.html

> This site has more than 2,500 activities.

Concepts to Classrooms

http://www.thirteen.org/edonline/concept2class

> The New York Public Broadcasting Concepts to Classrooms series has video demonstrating methods with teachers in classrooms.

The Smithsonian

http://www.si.edu

> The Smithsonian's resources span the humanities through the sciences and have both a teachers' and a kids' section.

Education World

http://www.educationworld.com

> This website might be described as the one-stop-shopping place for teachers. The number of resources is astounding. Educators will find articles and lesson plans, as well as links to other sites and international research. For teachers who are unsure of what

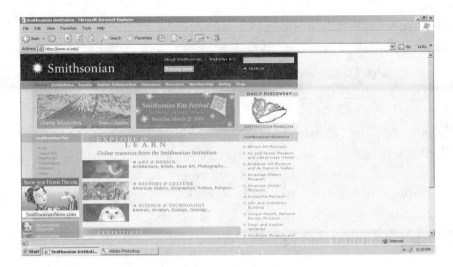

they hope to find on the Internet, Education World is a good place to start looking—but one should allow plenty of time for all the exploring opportunities available here.

Reprinted with permission of Karla Mickey.

EdHelper

http://www.edhelper.com

This site requires a subscription and provides lessons, grade-appropriate reading materials, worksheets, and assessments for multiple topics like the seasons, plants, and so forth.

Awesomelibrary

http://www.awesomelibrary.org

This site has a large number of reviewed lesson plans gleaned from multiple sites that are organized by subject field and grade level.

Critical Thinking Community

http://criticalthinking.org/resources/TRK12-strategy-list.shtml

This website is dedicated to helping teachers convert typically "low-level-thinking" lessons to critical thinking lessons.

MiddleWeb.com

http://www.middleweb.com/CurrStrategies.html

This site has many resources on social studies education.

Curriculum Achieve

http://www.buildingrainbows.com/CA/ca.home.php

This site is a collection of lesson plans by grade level, many of which offer thematic lesson planning opportunities.

Education Planet

http://www.educationplanet.com/

This site is a gateway to lesson plans and course materials cataloged by disciplines and categories that are more detailed than many other websites.

Sites for Teachers

http://sitesforteachers.com/index.html

This site has hundreds of websites for teachers rated by popularity.

Learning Page

http://lcweb2.loc.gov/learn/start/inres/index.html

This site is a gateway to lesson plans and course materials.

Marco Polo

http://www.marcopolo-education.org/index.aspx

This excellent site offers links to seven other websites: ArtsEdge (for arts education), EconLink (for economics education), EdSitement (for humanities education), Illuminations (for mathematics education), Read-Write-Think (for English), Science Netlinks (for science education), and Xpeditions (for geography education). Each of these sites is sponsored, and some were created, by well-known and respected educational organizations. Provided within each site are lesson plans that are standards-based for K–12 education.

The New York Times Learning Network

http://www.nytimes.com/learning/teachers/index.html

The *New York Times* offers this excellent website for teachers to use in the classroom. On this site are current news items (written in summary), but the site will take students beyond what they read. Teachers can link to hundreds of lesson plans for current and past events—there is a lesson plan archive—and are provided with ideas for interdisciplinary lessons as well. All lessons are standards-based, and the site offers links to information on standards. A daily current events quiz and links for parents and students are also included.

McREL

http://www.mcrel.com/resources/index.asp

This website is a part of McREL (Mid-continent Regional Education Laboratory). Standards and benchmarks are the main focus. Lesson plans on this site are listed by subject, and within each topic is a Related Content Standard link that details the standard associated with the lesson plan. Each standard is also described as primary, upper elementary, middle school/junior high, or high school, and can then be linked to a corresponding benchmark. Connections+ is excellent for teachers who need help in relating and citing standards and benchmarks in their lessons.

SCORE History/Social Science Online Resources

http://score.rims.k12.ca.us

SCORE (Schools of California Online Resources for Educators) is an excellent website that provides educators with links to numerous resources and lesson

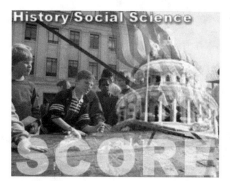

Reprinted with permission of Margaret A. Hill, Ph.D.

plans. Also included on this site is a link to California's frameworks, standards, and assessments. SCORE has two other links on its home page for Teacher Talk and Internet Classrooms, allowing opportunities for teachers and students to contact other teachers and classrooms.

Reprinted with permission of Cable in the Classroom CC/Crosby Publishing.

Cable in the Classroom

http://www.ciconline.org/home.htm

Cable in the Classroom is an initiative by the cable industry through which schools receive free cable service, including more than 540 hours per month of commercial-free educational programming. Highlights of the Cable in the Classroom website include Search the Listings, Curriculum Connections, and Professional Development Institute/Virtual Workshops. Search the Listings allows teachers to enter keywords or subjects and get lists of relevant curriculum-based programs airing with extended copyright clearances on 40 cable networks. Most networks have study guides and lesson plans available via the Internet; CICOnline also has links to all the network sites. Curriculum Connections focuses on how selected programs can be used to help students meet curriculum standards. Within the Professional Development Institute section, teachers can take virtual workshops, find links to top educational websites, and find the locations of upcoming hands-on workshops.

Before You Begin

The Internet is a tremendous resource for schools that facilitates research, education, communication, and entertainment. Moreover, it is a tool that is being accessed with increased frequency. The U.S. Department of Education reported in 2005 that nearly 100% of schools have the capacity to support online initiatives. In the very near future U.S. schools will have achieved universal access.

Although the online world offers many enriching opportunities for students, its expansive and global context still contains risks and potential dangers. Recognition of its disadvantages is necessary for making informed choices and managing risks with creative and commonsense solutions that promote safe and productive learning environments for children.

Although some of the Internet problems for schools are extensions of the common issues faced by parents when children access the Internet from home, schools also have unique issues that are specific to the educational setting. Common risks include potential interactions with cyberpredators who lure children for face-to-face encounters; exposure to content and information that is inappropriate for children, including pornography, violence, hate, misinformation, and hoaxes; access to products and information that may be used to harm them or others, such as guns, drugs, alcohol, and bomb-building recipes; harassment online with threats, insults, and the transmission of viruses; invasions of privacy and subsequent targeting for unfair marketing strategies; and scamming and defrauding through disclosure of financial information, such as credit card numbers and passwords. Schools also must address issues such as use of students' photos and personal information on school websites, plagiarism of Internet resources by students, student access to nonschool sites, the restriction of speech when online, students' skills in assessing the credibility of online resources, and informed consent of parents for their children's online activities at school.

Safety on the Internet depends on the education of administrators, teachers, parents, and students regarding procedures to promote well-being and minimize risk. Whether a child is first learning how to use a computer at school or is an experienced user of technology, educators have an opportunity to enhance children's safety before they become avid explorers of the wonders of cyberspace. By taking responsibility for children's online computer use, adults can greatly minimize any potential risks and assist children in experiencing the exciting global resources of the Internet.

The following guidelines are designed to create boundaries and barriers that promote safety:

1. The best way to assure that young people are having positive online experiences is to supervise their activities. Monitor students' computer activities and maintain open communication about information they have found, sites they have explored, and people with whom they have chatted. The FBI has created an online publication with guidelines on recognizing when a child is at risk online (http://www.fbi.gov/publications/pguide/pguidee.htm).

2. Investigate the use of filtering software. Several states have Internet-filtering laws that require public schools to adopt Internet use policies that prevent students from accessing sexually explicit, obscene, or harmful materials. Moreover, some states require the installation of filtering software on school computers. But even with these controls, responsible adults still need to be involved in monitoring students' use.

3. Establish an acceptable use policy for the Internet. The Internet Content Rating Association has developed a special "Children's Bill of Rights for the Internet" (http://www.icra.org/kids/billofrights/). Safekids.com (http://www.safekids.com/kidsrules.htm) has created a site that outlines suggested children's rules for online safety. These include basic rules, such as:
   a. Never give out identifying information (i.e., full name, home address, telephone number, age, race, family income, school name or location, or friends' names) online unless your parents have given you specific permission. Be sure that you are dealing with someone whom you and your parent or guardian know and trust before giving out any personal information. Also, remember that online information is not necessarily private.
   b. Never send a picture or video of yourself to another person without permission of your parent or guardian.
   c. When someone offers you gifts, money, or other promises of "something for nothing," tell your parent, guardian, or teacher.
   d. Tell your parent, guardian, teacher, or other trusted adult if you come across any information that makes you feel uncomfortable or confused. You should be especially cautious if messages imply secrecy or describe mechanisms for hiding information from parents, teachers, or other supervising adults. Do not respond to these messages, and end the communication immediately.
   e. Never arrange a face-to-face meeting unless your parent or guardian gives permission. If you have parental consent, make sure that you have a parent or guardian with you and arrange to meet in a public place.
   f. Remember that people online may not be who they say they are. Because you can't see or hear the person, it is easy for him or her to pretend to be someone else.

    g. Never use rude language or send mean messages. Treat other online users with respect.

    h. Do not give out credit card information without your parent's or guardian's permission.

    i. Never share your password, even with friends. When sites request a password, pick a different one than your log-on code.

The Internet can also be used by educators to assist them in understanding online risks and establishing rules and guidelines for safe web exploration by students. The following sites are a few links that will be helpful in this important area of promoting children's safety.

American Librarian Association Online Safety Rules and Suggestions

http://www.ala.org/ala/oif/foryoungpeople/childrenparents/especiallychildren.htm

The ALA offers online safety guidelines and numerous links to resources for children and parents.

Reprinted with permission of i-SAFE America.

i-SAFE America

http://www.isafe.org/

i-SAFE America, Inc. is a nonprofit foundation whose mission is to educate and empower youth to safely and responsibly take control of their Internet experiences. With bipartisan recognition and support from the United States Congress, i-SAFE has designed a proactive prevention-oriented Internet safety awareness program. Its website offers interactive classroom lessons, community outreach activities, and a youth empowerment campaign to link students, educators, parents, law enforcement, and community leaders in fostering the critical thinking and decision-making skills of youth when engaged in online experiences.

The CyberSmart! Curriculum

http://www.cybersmart.org/home/

The CyberSmart! Curriculum provides a comprehensive training for students K–8 which empowers them to use the Internet safely and responsibly. The curriculum includes 65 lessons that are correlated to the National Educational Technology Standards. Students acquire skills in safety, explore manners and responsible Internet use, focus on advertising and privacy online, examine the use of online resources for research, and reflect on technology in the past, present, and future. This valuable teaching resource can be downloaded free of charge from the website, and teachers or school districts can arrange for staff training on implementation of the curriculum through web-based, self-paced courses that are offered at reasonable prices with continuing education and college credit available.

Netsafe

http://www.netsafe.org.nz

The website of the Internet Safety Group of New Zealand offers information on various aspects of safety on the net. The organization has a downloadable kit for schools to guide them in establishing safe online educational experiences, and general information is provided on cybersecurity.

NetSmartz

http://www.netsmartz.org/

The National Center for Missing and Exploited Children and the Boys and Girls Clubs of America have created a resource with activities for kids as well as information for parents and educators, including interactive lesson plans for Internet safety and awareness.

National Cybersecurity Alliance

http://www.staysafeonline.org

The National Cybersecurity Alliance is sponsored by the Department of Homeland Security, the Federal Trade Commission, and many private-sector corporations and organizations. Its website offers cybersecurity tips, curriculum, and links to resources for educators to help teach children and young adults how to stay safe online.

Indiana Department of Education Acceptable Use Policy Links

http://www.doe.state.in.us/olr/aup/welcome.html

This site provides useful links to school acceptable use policies that may assist educators in developing and reevaluating their current communication of guidelines to parents and students for online access in school.

National Internet Fraud Watch Information Center

http://www.fraud.org/

Advice is available on scams in cyberspace, and guidelines are provided to help students identify and protect themselves from Internet fraud. Reports of suspected Internet fraud are directed to the appropriate authorities.

SafeKids

http://www.safekids.com/

This site allows access to the full text of Larry Magid's popular child safety and teen safety brochures.

Reprinted with permission of Parry Aftab.

WiredSafety and WiredKids

http://www.wiredsafety.org/

http://www.wiredkids.org/

Wired Safety and Wired Kids are sites that provide help, information, and education to Internet and mobile device users to prevent cybercrimes and abuses online. They provide support for cases of cyberabuse, ranging from identity and credential theft, online fraud and cyberstalking, to hacking and malicious code attacks. Interactive games and information resources are designed to help everyone learn how to protect their privacy and security online and to teach responsible Internet use.

ONLINE SIMULATIONS

Privacy Playground: The First Adventure of the Three Little CyberPigs (ages 7–9)

http://www.media-awareness.ca/english/special_initiatives/games/
privacy_playground/index.cfm

In this online game, students assist the Three Little CyberPigs in an adventure that introduces children to online marketing scams and privacy in cyberspace.

An accompanying teacher's guide provides lessons with activities and handouts for use in the classroom. All materials are available through a free download from the Media Awareness Network.

CyberSense and Nonsense: The Second Adventure of the Three CyberPigs (ages 9–11)

http://www.media-awareness.ca/english/special_initiatives/games/
cybersense_nonsense/index.cfm

In this adventure of the Three Little Cyberpigs, children learn the importance of validating online information and using rules of netiquette. The teacher guide and simulation can be downloaded from the Media Awareness Network.

Jo Cool or Jo Fool

http://www.media-awareness.ca/english/special_initiatives/games/
joecool_joefool/jo_cool_teachers.cfm

Media Awareness Network has created an online cybertour and quiz for more advanced students to test their cybersmarts. A comprehensive teacher's guide is also available.

Allies and Aliens

http://www.media-awareness.ca/english/games/allies_aliens/

The Media Awareness Network has designed this educational game for seventh- and eighth-grade students to develop their skills in identifying misinformation, prejudice, and propaganda online.

KidsCom Internet Safety Game

http://www.kidscom.com/games/isg/isg.html

This lively quiz game from KidsCom reviews basic Internet safety information with children.

Disney Surf Swell Island

http://disney.go.com/family/surfswell/

Disney designed this online adventure game to present Internet safety to elementary age students. A series of games featuring Disney characters focus on privacy, viruses, and netiquette. They also have incorporated information related to wireless technologies.

LEGAL AND ETHICAL ISSUES IN CYBERSPACE

The study of law and ethics facilitates an understanding of guidelines that direct our conduct and maintain the cohesiveness of our society. Thoughtful consideration of belief systems that contribute to the formulation of laws and policies can contribute to critical dialogue on morals, values, and constitutional liberties. These websites present a full range of contemporary legal and ethical issues that may aid in instruction on responsible behavior, individual rights, and the process of decision making when confronting dilemmas.

Computer Crime and Intellectual Property Section of the Criminal Division of the U.S. Department of Justice

http://www.usdoj.gov/criminal/cybercrime/parents.html

The U.S. Department of Justice has created a web page with resources and interactive materials to address cyberethics with youth. The page includes links to other cybersafety information, including a model acceptable use policy for IT resources in the schools.

Responsible Netizen

http://responsiblenetizen.org/

The Responsible Netizen site provides extensive information on young people's safe and responsible use of the Internet. The site includes access to online documents and publications that address emerging issues on legal decisions and efforts to promote ethical behavior in cyberspace.

Electronic Privacy Information Center

http://www.epic.org/

EPIC, located in Washington, D.C., describes itself as "a public interest research center" designed to alert the public to privacy and other civil liberty issues. It is a project of the Fund for Constitutional Government and works in association with other human rights groups. This site provides current news on policies affecting privacy and other constitutional privileges. Visitors can also view government documents obtained by EPIC through the use of the Freedom of Information Act.

Center for Democracy and Technology

http://www.cdt.org

This site provides visitors with a guide to pending federal legislation regarding issues such as free speech, data privacy, and cryptography. This nonprofit public interest organization focuses on the advancement of "democratic values and constitutional liberties in the digital age." Links to other resources, including state, national, and international organizations and government agencies, are also provided.

Kidz Privacy

http://www.ftc.gov/bcp/conline/edcams/kidzprivacy/index.html

The U.S. Federal Trade Commission site provides online privacy guidelines and resources for kids, parents, and educators. Information is presented about the Children's Online Privacy Protection Act.

National Center for Missing and Exploited Children (1-800-THE-LOST)

http://www.missingkids.com/cybertip

This private, nonprofit organization provides assistance to families of missing children and conducts prevention and awareness programs. A CyberTipline has been created in collaboration with the FBI, U.S. Postal Service, and Office of Juvenile Justice. When you come across child pornography on the web, you should report it by calling or contacting this site.

Netiquette Home Page

http://www.albion.com/netiquette/index.html

This site provides links to information about online manners, including an entire online book by Virginia Shea.

Institute for Global Ethics

http://www.globalethics.org/default.html

This organization promotes and educates about ethical decision making both on and off the Internet.

Cyberethics for Kids

http://www.cybercrime.gov/rules/kidinternet.htm

This resource is a site maintained by the U.S. Department of Justice's Computer Crime and Intellectual Property Section. It provides adults, children, and teens information on how to use the Internet safely and responsibly.

Cybercitizenship.org

http://www.cybercitizenship.org/index.html

Cybercitizenship.org provides approaches for teaching children about cyberethics. This site also includes sets of links for adults and children to help them gain a better understanding of the Internet.

United States Copyright Office

http://www.loc.gov/copyright/

The Copyright Office provides up-to-date news about copyright issues, as well as explaining the basics of copyright law.

Additional Cybersafety Websites

Bullying Online
http://www.bullying.co.uk/

Childnet International
http://www.childnet-int.org/

Connect for Kids
http://www.connectforkids.org/node/3116

Cyberbullying
http://www.cyberbullying.ca/

Cyber-Plagiarism
http://tlt.its.psu.edu/suggestions/cyberplag/

Information Literacy Primer
http://glef.org/tiliteracy.html

Internet Keep Safe Coalition
http://www.ikeepsafe.org/--index.php

Internet Super Heroes
http://www.internetsuperheroes.org/

Katiesplace.org
http://katiesplace.org/

KidSmart
http://www.kidsmart.org.uk/

Net Family News
http://netfamilynews.org/index.shtml

Sophos Anti-Virus Information
http://www.sophos.com/virusinfo/

Urban Legends Reference Page
http://www.snopes2.com/

DIGITAL LITERACY

Digital literacy represents the ability to access digital forms of information, critically evaluate its quality and utility, analyze information for connections to and expansions of knowledge, and use digital tools to produce original works. It emphasizes the capacity to fully participate as a responsible member of a technologically engaged society and refers to the skills that people need to understand and constructively navigate the digital media that surround them.

Due to the omnipresence of technology, adolescents require these critical reasoning skills to facilitate their active engagement with information. Digital literacy builds the foundation for productive functioning as a global citizen and addresses the development of skills needed for the evolving cyberdomain.

In order to foster the role of students as informed and participatory citizens, social studies teachers are increasingly integrating media literacy into their instruction. The following resources represent some of the best media literacy sites on the web.

Alliance for a Media Literate America

http://www.amlainfo.org/

The Alliance for a Media Literate America (AMLA) is a national, grassroots membership organization that is focused on media literacy education. Teaching guides and resources are available on the AMLA website that promote critical inquiry and skill building for students.

Center for Media Literacy

http://www.medialit.org/

The Center for Media Literacy offers a broad range of teaching materials for media literacy education, including books, videos, CD-based curriculum, teaching kits, and other forms of curriculum. It is the oldest and largest distributor of these materials for students in pre-K through college. It offers a CML MediaLit Kit™, which provides "a blueprint for building an inquiry-based media literacy program based on principles developed and honed through years of research and use both in the United States and around the world."

Media Education Foundation

http://www.mediaed.org

Thought-provoking video documentaries are produced and disseminated with printed discussion guides. The foundation's materials encourage critical thinking and debate about the relationship between media ownership, commercial media content, and the democratic demand for free flow of information, diverse representations of ideas and people, and informed citizen participation.

New Mexico Media Literacy Project

http://www.nmmlp.org/

Media literacy materials, including CD-ROMs, study guides, and other teaching resources, are available that explore the influence of media on young people through advertising.

Additional Media Literacy Websites

Action Coalition for Media Education
http://www.acmecoalition.org/

The Director in the Classroom
http://www.thedirectorintheclassroom.com/

Just Think
http://www.justthink.org/

Kids First—Coalition for Quality Children's Media
http://www.kidsfirst.org/

Listen Up! Youth Media Producers
http://www.pbs.org/merrow/listenup/

Media Literacy Clearinghouse
http://medialit.med.sc.edu/

Media Matters
http://mediamatters.org/

The National Institute on Media and the Family
http://www.mediafamily.org/

Project Look Sharp
http://www.ithaca.edu/looksharp/

CHAPTER **3**

United States History and Cultures

United States history involves an exploration of information concerned with American events that have taken place over time and continue to unfold, often focusing on the causes and effects of past events. The Internet offers many excellent sites that address various aspects of historical inquiry and encourage active learning.

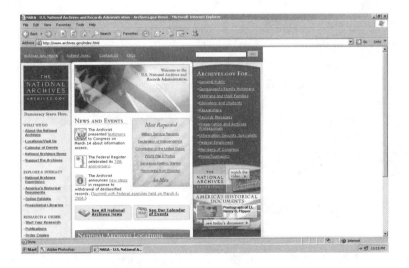

National Archives and Records Administration

http://www.archives.gov/index.html

Historical researchers may explore the *Federal Register* online as well as famous speeches and images. The Online Exhibit Hall contains primary source documents such as the Magna Carta and the Constitution. Primary source lesson plans and activities for teachers and students can be found in the Digital Classroom section of the site.

 II X

The Library of Congress

http://www.loc.gov

This recently updated site includes a number of exhibitions and American treasures from the collections of the Library of Congress. The American Memory section offers access to a large number of digitized historical collections in both audio and visual formats. When one enters the Library of Congress page, the site map assists in navigating this resource.

 II VI

America's Story from America's Library

http://www.americaslibrary.gov/cgi-bin/page.cgi

The Library of Congress presents "America's Library," a site created especially for children with a vast array of primary sources, such as letters, diaries, records and tapes, films, sheet music, maps, prints, photographs, and digital materials. The website also contains creative ways to learn about history through sections entitled "Meet Amazing Americans," "Jump Back in Time," "Explore the States," "Join America at Play," and "See, Hear and Sing."

 I II V X

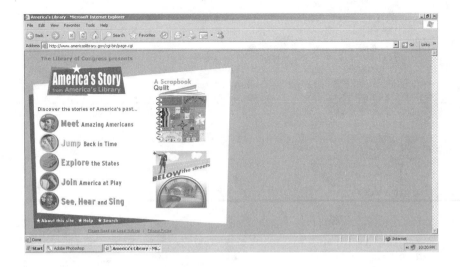

History Wired

http://historywired.si.edu

This site allows visitors to take a virtual tour of the Smithsonian Institution's objects of interest. The interactive site map enables visitors to search by selecting dates on a time line, selecting a broad category, or using a keyword search. Information is presented as though offered in a real-life tour with a Smithsonian curator.

 II V VI

The National Park Service

http://www.nps.gov

ParkNet provides links to the histories, cultures, and places of our nation's past. Information on Civil War battlefields, landmarks, and museum collections is just some of what you will find here. Questions about the National Parks, the National Park Service, or American history can be directed online to National Park Service historians.

 II III

National Women's History Museum

http://www.nmwh.org

An in-depth history of the American women's suffrage movement is presented. The site contains a time line of major events in the women's rights movement from the World Anti-Slavery Convention of 1840 through the passage of the Nineteenth Amendment. The online museum also contains an extensive image gallery and concluding interactive quiz about the site.

 II V VI X

THE
VALLEY
OF THE
S H A D O W

Two Communities in the American Civil War

Reprinted with permission of the Virginia Center for Digital History.

The Valley of the Shadow: Two Communities in the American Civil War

http://jefferson.village.virginia.edu/vshadow2

This hypermedia archive examines one Northern and one Southern community using the backdrop of the Civil War. The site contains thousands of sources, such as religious documents, photographs, military records, and maps. In the teaching materials section, teachers can find lesson plans for social studies classes grades 7–12, and students can find paper topics for high school and college United States history courses.

 II III

University of North Carolina at Chapel Hill's Documenting the American South

http://metalab.unc.edu/docsouth/

DocSouth provides a Southern perspective on American history and culture. There are a number of thematic collections of primary sources, including, "North American Slave Narratives," "The Southern Homefront, 1861–1865," "The Church in the Southern Black Community," and "First-Person Narratives of the American South." Teachers, students, and researchers will find a classroom resource section with a teacher toolkit and lesson plans related to information found on the website.

 II III

The History Channel

http://www.historychannel.com

Students can feel a personal connection to history by exploring "This Day in History," which provides information on Wall Street history, automotive history, Civil War history, and general history. The link "What Happened on Your Birthday?" allows people to find historical events and individuals connected to their birthday. The site also maintains a number of interactive exhibits on topics such as Ellis Island and "The Star Spangled Banner." Teachers from around the country who use the History Channel share ideas for lessons and projects.

 II

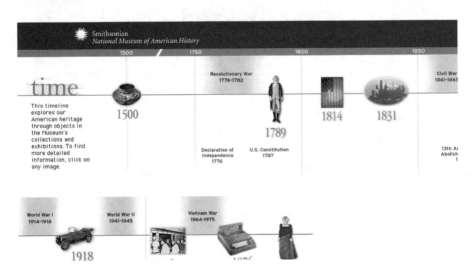

Smithsonian Institution National Museum of American History

http://americanhistory.si.edu/index.cfm

An interactive time line allows for exploration of American heritage through objects found in the museum's collections and exhibits. The site houses a wide array of virtual exhibitions spanning all aspects of American history. Some exhibitions have included "Edison after Forty," "Between a Rock and a Hard Place: A History of American Sweatshops, 1820–Present," and the "1896 Washington Salon & Art Photographic Exhibition." A highlight of the site is the interactive program "You Be the Historian." This link allows for the study of secondary and primary sources and facilitates historical processing skills.

 II

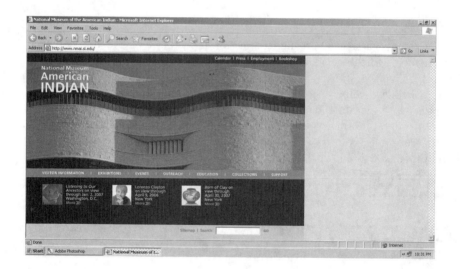

Smithsonian Institution National Museum of the American Indian

http://www.nmai.si.edu/

This site contains the NMAI Conexus that extends the walls of the museum through the World Wide Web. The NMAI Conexus shares the work of Native American artists with the public. Visitors can explore archives of past exhibits, various artists-in-residence, special events, and visiting artists.

 I II V

The History Place

http://www.historyplace.com/

Highlights include a historical photo and speech of the week. Students can find homework tips on how to write a better history paper. There is a comprehensive gallery of presidential portraits as well as sounds of the presidents. A presentation on child labor in America from 1908 to 1912 includes a number of primary source photographs.

 II

Core Documents of U.S. Democracy

http://www.gpoaccess.gov/coredocs.html

This site provides direct online access to current and historical government documents. These publications provide information about government activities and inform the electorate about the democratic process. This online forum allows for free and immediate access to authenticated versions of these core documents of democracy.

 II VI X

Additional U.S. History and Cultures Websites

50 States
http://www.50states.com

The Abraham Lincoln Presidential Library and Museum
http://www.alplm.org/intro.html

Archiving Early America
http://earlyamerica.com

Benjamin Franklin: A Documentary History
http://www.english.udel.edu/lemay/franklin/

Best of History Websites
http://besthistorysites.net/

Black History
http://www.kn.pacbell.com/wired/BHM/AfroAm.html

Center for History and New Media
http://chnm.gmu.edu/index1.html

The Civil War
http://www.pbs.org/civilwar/

The Civil War Home Page
http://www.civil-war.net/

Colonial Williamsburg
http://www.history.org/

Digital History
http://www.digitalhistory.uh.edu/

Discovery Channel American History Sites
http://www.discoveryschool.com/schrockguide/history/hista.html

Exploring Florida
http://fcit.usf.edu/florida/default.htm

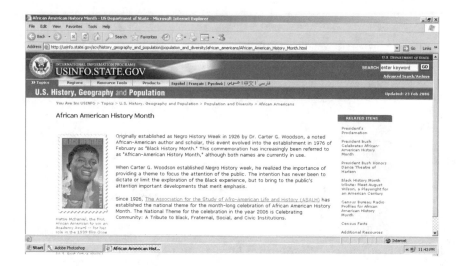

Gateway to African American History
http://usinfo.state.gov/usa/blackhis/

Great Chicago Fire and the Web of Memory
http://www.chicagohistory.org/fire/

Historical Text Archive African American History
http://historicaltextarchive.com/sections.php?op=listarticles&secid=8

Historical Text Archive Women's History
http://historicaltextarchive.com/links.php?op=viewlink&cid=20

In Motion: The African-American Migration Experience
http://www.inmotionaame.org/

Independence Hall Association
http://ushistory.org/

Lewis and Clark Expedition
http://www.pbs.org/lewisandclark/

Liberty! The American Revolution
http://www.pbs.org/ktca/liberty/index.html

The Library of Congress: Today in History
http://lcweb2.loc.gov/ammem/today/today.html

Mapping History
http://darkwing.uoregon.edu/~atlas/

MayflowerHistory.com
http://www.mayflowerhistory.com/

Memorial Hall Museum
http://memorialhall.mass.edu/home.html

National Constitution Center
http://www.constitutioncenter.org/

National Geographic Lewis and Clark
http://www.nationalgeographic.com/lewisandclark/

The National Underground Railroad Freedom Center
http://www.freedomcenter.org/

The New York Times on the Web Learning Network: American History
http://www.nytimes.com/learning/general/subjects/ushistory_index.html

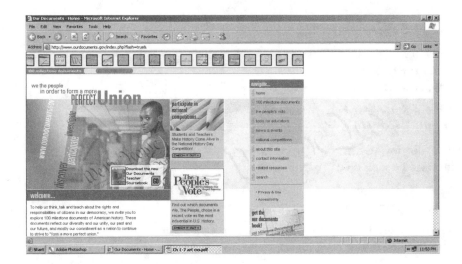

Our Documents
http://www.ourdocuments.gov/

Plimoth Plantation
http://www.plimoth.org/visit/what/index.asp

Raid on Deerfield: The Many Stories of 1704
http://www.1704.deerfield.history.museum/

*Schools of California Online Resources for Education,
History/Social Science*
http://score.rims.k12.ca.us/

The Smithsonian Center for Latino Initiatives
http://latino.si.edu/

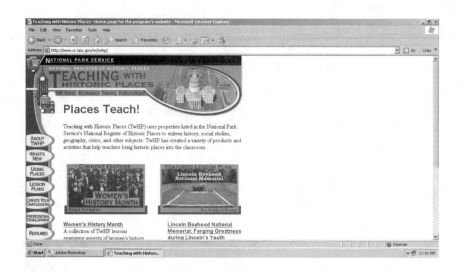

Teaching with Historic Places
http://www.cr.nps.gov/nr/twhp

United States Air Force Museum
http://www.wpafb.af.mil/museum/index.htm

The Virginia Center for Digital History
http://jefferson.village.virginia.edu/vcdh/

Virtual Jamestown
http://www.virtualjamestown.org/

Virtual Marching Tour of the American Revolution
http://www.ushistory.org/march/index.html

Wet with Blood: The Investigation of Mary Todd Lincoln's Cloak
http://www.chicagohistory.org/wetwithblood/

World History and Cultures

The World Wide Web (WWW) offers teachers of world history and cultures a dizzying array of sites that feature informational articles, accessible images, and virtual field trips to other countries and other time periods. General world history and cultures sites are listed first, followed by sites on specific regions of the world.

History Central

http://www.multied.com/dates/Index.html

Major historical events in the history of the world are identified, briefly discussed, and accompanied by relevant graphics and images.

 I II IX

Internet Modern History Sourcebook

**http://www.fordham.edu/halsall/mod/modsbookfull.html#
Scientific%20Revolution**

Full text of books, primary source documents, and official decrees can be found on this website. They are arranged chronologically and thematically. Also available are thousands of resources, links, and multimedia (video clips, pictures, and audio) on a variety of historical topics and epochs such as ancient, African, Islamic, Jewish, and women's history.

 I II IX

World History Compass

http://www.worldhistorycompass.com

Hundreds of links to the history of every region of the world, both past and present.

 I II IX

Mr. Don's World History Resources

http://members.aol.com/MrDonnHistory/World.html

This excellent gateway site covers traditional topics such as the history of specific time periods, events, and people. Contemporary topics such as terrorism and women's history are also included. Truly novel are options for time lines, world holidays, and free worksheets, as well as links to online services and other resources about history.

 I II IX

Mr. Dowling.com

http://www.mrdowling.com

Topics on this teacher-friendly site range from prehistory to contemporary regions and conflicts. Clicking on each topic gives you a thumbnail sketch and historical overview. There are also hundreds of complementary free lesson plans, study guides, homework assignments, and exams. A helpful feature is that users can edit the lesson plans online before printing.

 I II III IX

Visual History Foundation

http://www.vhf.org

The Visual History Archive contains thousands of videotaped testimonies from Holocaust survivors and other witnesses. Not only is it the largest archive of its kind, but each testimony has been cataloged with keywords for accessibility. The Foundation's mission is to overcome prejudice, intolerance, and bigotry through the educational use of the archive's visual history testimonies. In addition to the interactive, visual exhibits, teachers can download lesson plans and stream video clips. The student section features a time line, a glossary, and links to additional resources.

 II III IX

Histor eSearch

http://www.snowcrest.net/jmike

Intended for both students and educators, this is a comprehensive site featuring hundreds of links to sites related to modern and ancient world history, medieval history, Latin American history, and African history, among others.

 I II IX X

BBC Modern World History

http://www.bbc.co.uk/history

This site maintained by the British Broadcasting Corporation features interactive animations, including animated maps and time lines (animation requires Shockwave software, which is available on the site). The teachers' section provides lessons, further resources, and links to related sites.

 I II IX

The History Channel

http://www.historychannel.com

In addition to articles, historic speeches, and video clips, this site offers hundreds of links to other history-related sites. Students will enjoy the "What Happened on Your Birthday?" feature, and teachers will find study guides, quizzes, and teaching ideas in "Classroom."

 I II IX

MiddleWeb History and Social Studies Resources

http://www.middleweb.com/CurrSocStud.html

This gateway site provides access to a number of world history links. Topics include the origins of humankind, a virtual autopsy of a preserved Incan, ancient and medieval history, and teaching about the Holocaust.

 I II IX

Kathy Schrock's Guide for Educators: World and Ancient History

http://discoveryschool.com/schrockguide/history/histw.html

This excellent site should be the first place world history teachers visit. In addition to extensively covering virtually all related topics, it offers useful features and information such as lesson plans, web links, discussions, and images.

History/Social Studies Website for K–12 Teachers

http://home.comcast.net/~dboals1/boals.html

Provides assistance to K–12 teachers in locating WWW resources for the teaching of history. Topics include archaeology, European history, non-Western history, and the humanities and art. The non-Western history sites section features comprehensive links for the study of Asia, Africa, Central and South America, the Middle East, India, and others.

Awesome Library: K–12 Social Studies Lesson Plans

http://www.awesomelibrary.org/social.html

Topics include general history resources, multicultural activities, and multidisciplinary lessons. Particularly useful is the breakdown for elementary teachers, for teens, and for secondary teachers.

EDSITEment

http://edsitement.neh.fed.us

Sponsored in part by the National Endowment for the Humanities, this site includes lesson plans, learning guides, and links to the top humanities sites on the web. Of particular interest are the links to top museums, libraries, and cultural institutions.

Tales of Wonder

http://www.darsie.net/talesofwonder

This award-winning collection of folk and fairy tales has representative stories from virtually all countries of the world and underscores humanity's common heritage of storytelling.

 I II IX

World History Archives

http://www.hartford-hwp.com/archives

This gateway site offers documents and images from ancient to contemporary times. In addition to broad topics such as politics and war, the economy, and the environment, users can access documents by world region.

 I II IX

Exploring Ancient World Cultures

http://eawc.evansville.edu

This introduction to ancient world cultures on the WWW begins with an excellent essay entitled "Why Study Ancient World Cultures?" useful in developing a rationale for students. Topics include the Near East, India, Egypt, China, Greece, Rome, Islam, and Europe.

 I II IX

Ancient World History: Omaha Public Library

http://www.omahapubliclibrary.org/subjects/society/history/
historymain.html

Teachers of young students will find helpful information, lesson plans, and links in this site. In particular, connections to literature, virtual activities, and information about daily life topics (such as toys, pets, clothing, and hairstyles) are useful tools.

 I II IX

HyperHistory Online

http://www.hyperhistory.com

A collection of time lines that graphically display 3,000 years of world history. The organization allows viewers to compare the relationships among people, places, and events throughout history. Interlinked maps provide geographic context. Users can also link to more than 300 related websites.

 I II IX

A Teacher's Guide to the Holocaust

http://fcit.coedu.usf.edu/holocaust

Classroom activities, web links, music, photographs, and art are just some of the resources available on this impressive site.

 I II IX

Art History Resources on the Web

http://witcombe.bcpw.sbc.edu/ARTHLinks.html

The study of history can be greatly enhanced by the inclusion of art. This site has links to galleries and resources, and users can even access images of art produced in prehistoric times through the twentieth century.

I II IX

Portals to the World

http://www.loc.gov/rr/international/portals.html

This Library of Congress portal website leads users to electronic resources for every country in the world.

II III IX

Globalization 101

http://www.globalization101.org

Although this website focuses on current events and issues, many of the "briefs" provide a good historical background that contextualizes contemporary events.

 II IX

AFRICA AND THE MIDDLE EAST

Middle East Network Information Center

http://menic.utexas.edu/mes.html

In addition to a country index, users can access contents by subject (such as ancient history, arts and humanities, religion, and energy). Teachers will find useful the K–12 educational resources and electronic publishing features.

 I II III IX

K–12 Electronic Guide for African Resources on the Internet

http://www.sas.upenn.edu/African_Studies/Home_Page/AFR_GIDE.html

Maintained by the University of Pennsylvania's African Studies Center, this site features an annotated listing of resource-full sites for use in the study and teaching of Africa. In addition to country-by-country information, there is information about the history, languages, and environment of Africa. Especially useful for educators is the multimedia archives section, which features maps and satellite images, flags, and photographs.

 I II III IX

H-Afrteach

http://www.h-net.msu.edu/~afrteach

This discussion list caters to educators and students interested in African studies. In addition to lesson plans, course syllabi, and other instructional materials, users can access images, folktales, and timely book reviews.

 I II IX

Africa-Related Links

http://africa.wisc.edu/links

The University of Wisconsin–Madison's African Studies Program provides hundreds of links to resources on the WWW. Topics include news, politics, art, languages, literature, and more. Of special interest to educators is the K–12 Resources and Instructional Materials section.

 I II IX

Little Horus

http://www.horus.ics.org.eg/en/Default_HTML.aspx

This site is especially appropriate for elementary school students. Users take a tour of Egypt, where they learn about its history, geography, and entertainment. The bilingual site (English and Arabic) boasts more than 3,000 pages of text and graphics.

 I II III IX

USAID Bureau for Africa

http://www.usaid.gov/locations/sub-saharan_africa/index.html

Contains information on development activities in Africa. For educators and students, the most helpful features present country-by-country data, the status of education, and environmental concerns.

 I II III IX

African Studies Internet Resources

http://www.columbia.edu/cu/libraries/indiv/area/Africa/index.html

This web page on the Columbia University libraries' site provides a wealth of resources and links for both students and teachers. Resources are broken down by region and country, organizations, and topics. Teaching resources include K–12 curriculum materials.

I II III IX

ASIA AND THE PACIFIC

Ask Asia

http://www.askasia.org

Multimedia site on a wide range of topics related to the history, culture, and politics of Asia. Includes lessons, images, photos, and maps that can be downloaded and used in K–12 classrooms. Also provides a link to Asia Source, a searchable database on current events in the region.

 I II III IX

Asian Studies WWW Virtual Library

http://coombs.anu.edu.au/WWWVL-AsianStudies.html

Exhaustive annotated listings and links to resources on the region as a whole and on individual countries and topics. Users can also access information by the individual country and territory listings.

 I II IX

India and China in Comparative and Global Perspective

http://www.intranet.csupomona.edu/~inch/welcome.html

Showcases curriculum projects created by teachers involved in a 3-year professional development program on India and China. Links to selected Internet sites about Asia are also provided.

 I II IX

China on the Net

http://www.kn.pacbell.com/wired/China/hotlist.html

Comprehensive list of Internet links for the study of China. Students will appreciate learning pages like Treasure Hunt, Multimedia Scrapbook, and Web Quest. Features include virtual tours, Chinese culture and proverbs, religions, human rights, the environment, and the visual arts. "Searching for China" is a role-playing/simulation activity that teaches students about the complexities of the country.

 I II III IX

Pacific Internet Sites

http://www.nla.gov.au/oz/pacsites.html

Links to reference material, news sources, electronic journals, and more—all related to the Pacific.

 I II IX

Pacific Islands Internet Resources

http://www2.hawaii.edu/~ogden/piir/index.html

Links to WWW resources focusing on the Pacific Islands, including media resources, document collections, maps, and images.

 I II IX

EUROPE

Multnomah County Library

http://www.multcolib.org/homework/eurohist.html

Extensive collection of links to European history topics and images. The 3,500 K–12 resources were reviewed and selected by educators and librarians. Topics include medieval history, rulers, speeches, and biographies.

 I II IX

The Holocaust World Resource Center

http://www.hwrc.org

This nonprofit educational site is an international center for Holocaust resources. Different areas related to Eastern European Jewry are included.

 I II IX

Academic Info: European History

http://www.academicinfo.net/histeuro.html

This site offers links to specific topics such as Spanish history, World War I, and the Cold War, as well as portals to megasites on European history.

 I II III IX

WWW Virtual Library: West European Studies

http://www.library.pitt.edu/subject_guides/westeuropean/wwwes/

Comprehensive guide to Internet resources on Western Europe. The search engine allows for searches by academic discipline. Also included are regional current events.

 I II IX

Yale University Library: European History and West European Studies

http://www.library.yale.edu/Internet/eurohist.html

A variety of links to electronic resources concerning the history of Europe.

 I II IX

Revelations from the Russian Archives

http://lcweb.loc.gov/exhibits/archives/intro.html

Unique Library of Congress site focusing on twentieth-century Russia. Lots of information on the internal workings of the Soviet system and its relations with the United States.

 I II IX

USAID Regions: Europe and Eurasia

http://www.info.usaid.gov/regions/eni

Links to information on all the countries in Europe and the former Soviet Union.

 I II IX

The Holocaust: A Learning Site for Students

http://www.ushmm.org/outreach

The U.S. Holocaust Memorial Museum's site provides students and teachers with text, maps, historical photographs and images of artifacts, and audio clips. The detailed visual time line facilitates student understanding of how events unfolded.

I II IX

LATIN AMERICA AND THE CARIBBEAN

Handbook of Latin American Studies

http://lcweb2.loc.gov/hlas

Annotated bibliography on Latin America. Updated monthly, it provides access to all volumes since its first publication in 1935.

 I II IX

Hispanic Reading Room

http://www.loc.gov/rr/hispanic

This Library of Congress site features catalogs of Hispanic materials and collections. The Ask a Librarian allows users to send reference staff a question about the collections, resources, and services.

 I II IX

LANIC: Primary and Secondary Education

http://www1.lanic.utexas.edu/la/region/k–12/

The Latin American Network Information Center provides information about every country in the region. On this trilingual site you can find data regarding the humanities, the economy, society and culture, and sustainable development, among the many topics covered.

 I II III IX

WWW Virtual Library: Latin American Studies

http://lanic.utexas.edu/las.html

Excellent database of resources and links about Latin American studies. Users can select specific countries or access information by subject. The K–12 feature is particularly helpful for educators.

 I II IX

Latin World

http://www.latinworld.com

A directory of Internet resources on Latin America and the Caribbean. Although a large part of this bilingual site focuses on trade and commerce, information on cultural traditions, history, and government is also provided. The search engine facilitates access to data and images. Latin World Kids provides links to educational, arts and literature, and "ask the expert" sites.

 I II IX

USAID Regions: Latin America and the Caribbean

http://www.usaid.gov/locations/latin_america_caribbean

Information on selected countries in Latin America and the Caribbean. Most useful is the current information on social and economic indicators.

 I II III IX

SICE: Foreign Trade Information Service

http://www.sice.oas.org

Maintained by the Organization of American States, this trilingual site offers the latest information on international trade issues. The "site map" provides detailed, country-specific data on all members of the OAS.

 I II IX

Americas Society

http://www.americas-society.org

Resources and information about the Western Hemisphere (including Canada, Latin America, and the Caribbean), especially in the arts, literature, and music.

 I II IX

Additional World History and Cultures Websites

Africa Quest
http://africaquest.classroom.com

AfroCuba Web
http://afrocubaweb.com

Art and Life in Africa Project
http://www.uiowa.edu/~africart

Atlas of the Greek and Roman World
http://www.unc.edu/depts/cl_atlas

Collapse: Why Do Civilizations Fall?
http://www.learner.org/exhibits/collapse

Encyclopedia Mythica
http://www.pantheon.org

The Great War
http://www.pbs.org/greatwar

History On-Line
http://www.historian.org

K–12 History on the Internet Resource Guide
http://www.xs4all.nl/~swanson/history

Perseus Digital Project
http://www.perseus.tufts.edu

Polynesian Cultural Center
http://www.polynesia.com

Religious History
http://www.georgetown.edu/labyrinth/subjects/relig/relig.html

Renaissance: What Inspired This Age of Balance and Order?
http://www.learner.org/exhibits/renaissance

Social Studies School Service Ancient History
http://socialstudies.com/c/@0/Pages/ancienthistory.html

Springfield Township High School Virtual Library: World History
http://mciunix.mciu.k12.pa.us/~spjvweb/stuworld.html

WWW-VL History: Central Catalogue
http://www.ukans.edu/history/VL

CHAPTER 5

Government and Law

The best way to study how government works is by watching the government itself in action. The World Wide Web (WWW) now gives direct access to national, state, and local government agencies, where students and teachers can both observe and participate in government activities online.

National Archives and Records Administration (NARA)

http://www.archives.gov/index.html

The National Archives, the official repository of U.S. government documents, provides a treasure trove of material for teaching government and history. The Online Exhibit Hall shows hundreds of original documents as diverse as the Declaration of Independence, the Constitution of the United States of America, World War II posters, and "When Nixon Met Elvis." The Research Room provides excellent guidance on searching and obtaining NARA's vast library of documents, and the Digital Classroom provides primary source documents and instructional activities employing materials from the National Archives. High-interest documents (such as the *Apollo* 11 flight plan) are featured monthly, along with instructional materials and research tips. From NARA's website, each of the U.S. presidential libraries is just one click away.

 II IV VI X

Thomas

http://thomas.loc.gov

Thomas, a huge and successful undertaking of the Library of Congress, provides full access to legislative information on the Internet. This vast site includes the text of bills before Congress, voting records of legislators, records of committee activity, the full text of the *Congressional Record*, and hundreds of other resources for students of government and their teachers. This is a one-stop resource for information about the functioning of the legislative branch of the U.S. government.

 II V VI X

White House for Kids

http://www.whitehouse.gov/kids/

Whitehousekids.gov is an educational opportunity for young Americans to learn about the White House and the president through fun and exciting features. This guide gives teachers ideas on how to use the site in the classroom and parents ideas on topics to discuss with their children as they navigate through the site.

 II V VI X

U.S. Citizenship and Immigration Services

http://uscis.gov/graphics/index.htm

Information and primary resources that help individuals learn about civics in the United States are highlighted in this website. Easily accessible instructional materials include *Welcome to the United States: A Guide for New Immigrants*, civic flash cards, short lessons, and a video tribute to America's history as a nation of immigrants. An extensive list of federal websites and a glossary of relevant terms may assist students as they engage in research projects.

 V VI X

FirstGov

http://www.firstgov.gov/

This portal site is a gateway to all government agencies and services for citizens and businesses. It includes federal, state, local and tribal agencies and provides access to everything from passport applications and social security information to lottery results. It is literally a "first stop" in dealing with the government.

 VI X

Landmark Supreme Court Cases

http://www.landmarkcases.org

This site was developed to provide teachers with a full range of resources and activities to support the teaching of landmark Supreme Court cases, helping students explore the key issues of each case. Estimates of each case's reading level help teachers plan for use with different grade levels and student groups.

 VI X

Keeping America Informed

http://www.access.gpo.gov

Virtually every piece of paper the government produces is printed by the U.S. Government Printing Office. Most of the recent materials are available online with full instructions for downloading them on a personal computer. Others are available at very low cost. Topics include the 9-11 Commission Report, economic indicators, and the entire federal budget. Search and browse features make this an easy site to use. Go to GPO Access to find materials.

 VI X

Superintendent of Documents, U.S. Government Printing Office; http://bensguide.gpo.gov/

Ben's Guide to the U.S. Government for Kids

http://bensguide.gpo.gov/

This engaging portal site provides kids with access to the government agencies that will be useful to them for school or community projects. It covers such topics as Our Nation, Historical Documents, Branches of Government, How Laws Are Made, and many more in an attractive, kid-friendly, format.

 VI X

Fed World Information Network

www.fedworld.gov

A project of the U.S. Department of Commerce, Fed World is an information network that links you to thousands of federal resources on the Internet. This is a great place for students to check out the federal jobs that are available anywhere in the nation.

 V VI X

Archiving Early America

http://earlyamerica.com

This site provides high-quality digital primary source material from eighteenth-century America. Original newspapers, maps, and writings are shown on the computer screen much as they appeared more than 200 years ago. This is a must-visit site for teachers interested in document analysis approaches to social studies.

 II VI X

Avalon Project at the Yale Law School: Documents in Law, History and Diplomacy

http://www.yale.edu/lawweb/avalon/avalon.htm

This award-winning site provides full-text documents that are foundational to the study of American democracy, from the Code of Hammurabi (B.C. 1750) to a collection of documents related to the 9-11 attack on the United States (2001). This site is truly astonishing for its depth and ease of use.

 I V VI X

Additional Government Websites

Infoplease from Lycos on U.S. Government and History
http://infoplease.lycos.com/ipa/A0101021.html

The Educator's Reference Desk from the Creators of "Ask ERIC Lesson Plans"
http://www.eduref.org/

EXECUTIVE BRANCH

The executive branch of the federal government consists of the offices of the president and vice president, cabinet officers, and all their respective departments, bureaus, and agencies.

The White House

http://www.whitehouse.gov

Not only is the White House the home of the president of the United States, but it is also the seat of the executive branch of the government. This site gives rich information about the offices of the president and vice president, the history of these offices, and the story of the White House itself as a historical building. There is also a feature page on the First Lady and a section on the family living quarters.

 II V VI X

U.S. Department of State

http://www.state.gov

The Department of State's website offers a rich array of resources on America's foreign policy and relations with foreign governments. One of the most visited sections includes travel warnings and consular information sheets. Warnings sheets provide snapshots of some of the world's most troubled nations and regions, and consular information sheets give details on immigration practices, health issues, political disturbances, currency regulations, crime and security, drug information, and the stability of government services for every nation in the world. New features include podcasts and listservs on the State Department's activity.

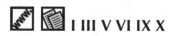 I III V VI IX X

Federal Bureau of Investigation

http://www.fbi.gov

The FBI page offers valuable information about crime investigation in the United States and how the federal agency assists local police in solving crimes. The

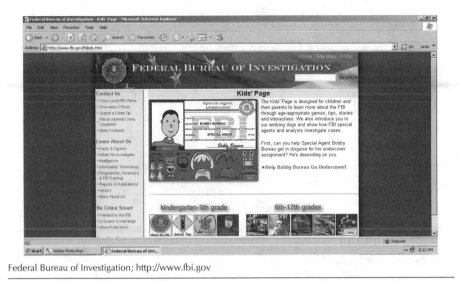

Federal Bureau of Investigation; http://www.fbi.gov

famous "Ten Most Wanted" list is available on this site, as are stories of major ongoing investigations. The "FBI for Kids" page features information on crime detection and crime prevention, as well as games and activities related to law enforcement. Age-appropriate games, lessons, and features cover topics such as fingerprints, crime-fighting dogs, and the chemistry of crime. Special links are provided for teachers and parents to other educational websites as well.

 V VI VII X

U.S. Department of Justice

http://www.usdoj.gov/kidspage

The Department of Justice's Justice for Kids & Youth website is an informative resource on the courts and the law, crime prevention, and civil rights. In addition to providing special features for children, this site links teachers and parents to instructional resources on topics such as tolerance, health and safety, and current events, as well as topics linked specifically to social studies: criminology, human relations, government, technology, and history.

 V VI VIII X

Central Intelligence Agency (CIA)

http://www.cia.gov/cia/ciakids/index.shtml

The CIA's *World Fact Book* is a veritable textbook for area studies, geopolitics, and contemporary world history. Entries for every nation contain current maps and information on the geography, people, government, economy, communications, transportation, and military, as well as transnational issues. In a world where borders and alliances change daily, the *Fact Book* alone would be worth a visit, but there is even more. Games include "Try a Disguise," "Code Warriors," and word puzzles. There is a colorful history of espionage, intelligence, and the agency and a special feature on the CIA's Canine Corps. A link back to the CIA main page leads to more sophisticated information for older students, including instructions for obtaining "declassified" intelligence documents.

 I III V VI VIII IX X

U.S. Census Bureau

http://www.census.gov

The Census Bureau website provides access to the most comprehensive statistical information imaginable about the United States and its people. Users can search for and arrange data in ways that answer specific questions about conditions and trends in the United States. Especially helpful for teachers is the site's Gazetteer, with map-drawing capability for any site in the United States included in the Census, from Los Angeles, California, to Ten Sleep, Wyoming. Go to "For Teachers" for teaching materials and publications suitable for use in K–12 classrooms.

 I III V VI X

Additional Executive Branch Websites

U.S. Department of Agriculture
http://www.usda.gov

U.S. Department of Commerce
http://www.doc.gov

U.S. Department of Defense
http://www.defenselink.mil

U.S. Department of Education
http://www.ed.gov

U.S. Department of Energy
http://www.energy.gov

U.S. Department of Health and Human Services
http://www.dhhs.gov

U.S. Department of Housing and Urban Development
http://www.hud.gov

U.S. Department of the Interior
http://www.doi.gov

U.S. Department of Labor
http://www.dol.gov

U.S. Department of Transportation
http://www.dot.gov

U.S. Department of Veterans Affairs
http://www.va.gov

U.S. Office of Management and Budget
http://www.whitehouse.gov/OMB

LEGISLATIVE BRANCH

The legislative branch of the federal government consists of the House of Representatives and the Senate. Both bodies provide excellent resources for the study of government and the legislative process.

U.S. House of Representatives

http://www.house.gov

The House site gives access to congressional representatives, as well as information about current deliberations and votes. Linked to the home page is an excellent document on "The Legislative Process" and the protocols and operations of the House.

 V VI X

U.S. House of Representatives: Educational Resources

http://www.house.gov/house/Educate.shtml

A special section of the House of Representatives website provides educational resources on the legislative process, how laws are made, the Declaration of Independence, and the Constitution, as well as historical information about the House and its role in the Republic.

II V VI X

U.S. Senate

http://www.senate.gov

Contact a senator, track a presidential nomination, follow the activity on the Senate floor, or check on committee activity on this attractive and well-designed

U.S. Senate; http://www.senate.gov

website. Students and teachers can also find interesting and engaging materials on the history of the Senate, its art collection, and myths and falsehoods about the Senate and its members, past and present. Click on Learning About the Senate to explore the Senate's legislative process, check out frequently asked questions, or e-mail a question to the Senate historian or curator.

 II V VI X

JUDICIAL BRANCH

The judicial branch of government is made up of the Supreme Court and all other courts in the federal system. Because federal, state, and local court systems are linked by the appeals process, the resources in this section are selected to provide social studies teachers with information about all levels of the legal system in the United States.

U.S. Supreme Court

http://www.supremecourtus.gov/

The court's site provides an excellent history of the court, a full docket of its upcoming cases, oral arguments presented by opposing sides, and dozens of other interesting features.

 V VI X

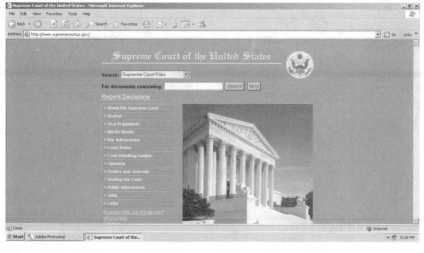

U.S. Supreme Court; http://www.supremecourtus.gov

Oyez Project: Northwestern University

http://www.oyez.org/oyez/frontpage

The Oyez Project is one of the most comprehensive resources imaginable on the Supreme Court of the United States. It provides full-text versions of written arguments, decisions, and dissenting opinions. Most intriguing are the recordings of actual oral arguments, which can be heard through the computer's sound system using Real Audio®. This is a vast, attractive, and interactive site that allows teachers to explore this very serious and important content in a manageable way.

 V VI X

Legal Information Institute: Cornell University Law School

http://www.law.cornell.edu

This comprehensive search site provides access to a vast array of resources for legal scholars, students, and teachers. Its sophisticated search capacity links users to laws about virtually any topic affecting contemporary life and provides excellent coverage of U.S. Supreme Court decisions as well as state and local court opinions. One of its most interesting features for social studies teachers is access to constitutional and legal information from nations around the globe.

 V VI IX X

FindLaw

http://www.findlaw.com

FindLaw is focused on law and government and provides access to a comprehensive, growing library of legal resources useful to legal professionals, teachers, consumers, and small businesses. FindLaw's mission is to make legal information on the Internet easy to find. For teachers and students, this site provides access to legal information on hundreds of topics, as well as information about legal careers and legal help for families and community members.

 V VI X

National Law Related Education Resource Center

http://www.abanet.org/publiced/resources/home.html

The National Law Related Education Resource Center provides an excellent gateway to dozens of Internet resources for law-related education for children and youth. From this site, teachers can order the *LRE Report*, the nation's leading newsletter on issues, trends, and people in law-related education.

 V VI X

Court TV Online

http://www.courttv.com

Sometimes controversial, often provocative, but always an engaging and intriguing look at contemporary legal issues, trials, and crime. This commercial site provides background information and up-to-the-minute reporting on current legal proceedings (mostly criminal cases), along with interviews of key players in high-profile cases, blunt commentary, and debates by legal experts in specialized fields. This site is most suitable for adults and older students. It includes instructional materials for teachers and a viewing guide and schedule.

 V VI X

Office of Juvenile Justice and Delinquency Prevention (OJJDP): U.S. Department of Justice

http://ojjdp.ncjrs.org

The OJJDP website is designed to provide information and resources on juvenile crime and communities' work to create safe environments for children and youth. Click on "Are you a student?" to find the most useful resources for secondary classrooms.

 V VI X

American Civil Liberties Union (ACLU)

http://www.aclu.org

The Constitution authorizes the government to act, and the Bill of Rights limits that ability in very specific ways. The ACLU is a public interest organization devoted exclusively to protecting the basic civil liberties guaranteed in the Bill of Rights. In its almost seven decades in existence, the ACLU has become a national institution; its website reflects its long history and its complex, and often controversial, agenda. From a strictly rights-oriented point of view, the ACLU site offers resources and commentary on dozens of the most difficult legal issues facing this nation, including the Patriot Act, abortion, gay rights, the death penalty, racial equality, students' rights, and privacy. It is direct, forthright, and uncompromising. Older students love it.

 V VI X

Street Law

www.streetlaw.org

An outgrowth of Georgetown University's practical law program, first taught in Washington, D.C., schools more than 20 years ago, Street Law is a "nonprofit organization dedicated to empowering people through law related education." It offers instructional materials and student texts, as well as information about the legal system to educators at all levels of the system.

 V VI X

National Crime Prevention Council

http://www.ncpc.org

The group that brought us McGruff, the crime-fighting dog, sponsors this lively website, which contains very helpful information about crime awareness and community involvement in crime prevention. A new focus on school safety and safe behavior in the community is particularly helpful for younger children, and the council's crime watch programs are often used as public service projects for older students.

 V VI X

Additional Law and Court Website

Emory Law Library Federal Courts Finder
http://www.law.emory.edu/FEDCTS

LOCAL GOVERNMENT

Most experience with government is at the local level. These sites put teachers and students in touch with both state and local governments.

States' News

http://www.csg.org/CSG/default.htm

Produced and updated weekly by the Council of State Governments, this very informative site covers government activity in all the states, possessions, and territories. Especially interesting is its coverage of the effects of federal legislation and mandates on state and local governments. From this helpful site, students and teachers can follow links to websites for all 50 states, Guam, and Puerto Rico.

 V VI X

State and Local Governments

http://www.loc.gov/rr/news/stategov/stategov.html

A service of the Library of Congress, this site offers a comprehensive catalog of links to state and local government resources, including state maps and links to the websites of state and local government agencies.

 V VI X

INTERNATIONAL AFFAIRS AND ORGANIZATIONS

National governments attempt to secure their mutual defense, promote peace, and assist in the development of all world nations through international organizations. For the United States, two of the most important of these agencies are the North Atlantic Treaty Organization (NATO) and the United Nations (UN).

United Nations

http://www.un.org

The website provides access to information about the UN's history and achievements, as well as its ongoing programs in peace and security, international law, humanitarian affairs, human rights, and economic and social development.

Online full-text documents allow students to track UN peacekeeping and relief missions, and high-quality maps are provided for each of the member countries and the UN mission sites.

 II III V VI IX

UNICEF—Voices of Youth

http://www.unicef.org/voy

The United Nations International Children's Emergency Fund (UNICEF) provides Voices of Youth, an informative and engaging opportunity to help students develop awareness of issues and crises confronting children and youth throughout the world. The Meeting Place gives students a chance to interact with other young people around the world through a bulletin board system that often carries powerful and wrenching messages from children in warring or disaster-torn countries. The Learning Place is an online resource students can use to learn about world issues and crises, and the Teachers' Place provides instructional materials and guidance for teachers who wish to explore the rights of children in their classes.

 I III V VI IX

Foreign Affairs Guide to International Affairs on the Internet

http://www.foreignaffairs.org/WAClinks.html

This venerable journal's website serves as an easy-to-navigate portal to one of the most comprehensive listings of international affairs links on the Internet. It includes news services and international news agencies, think tanks and advocacy groups, and international organizations. This is an excellent first stop for teacher and student research on foreign affairs.

 I II V VI IX

International Court of Justice

http://www.icj-cij.org/icjwww/igeneralinformation/icjgnnot.html

The International Court of Justice (ICJ), which has its seat in The Hague, is the principal judicial organ of the United Nations. The court has a dual role: to settle in accordance with international law the legal disputes submitted to it by states, and to give advisory opinions on legal questions referred to it by duly authorized international organizations and agencies. In recent years, it has tried cases ranging fromthe violation of trade treaties to crimes against humanity and ethnic cleansing.

 V VI IX X

WWW Virtual Library: International Affairs Resource— Elizabethtown College

http://www.etown.edu/vl

This superb website provides access to new resources, including live international radio and television broadcasts, organizations such as the European Union and the United Nations, regional and national information, and information on global issues such as the environment, development, and human rights. This is a genuine foundational resource for the study of international affairs in social studies.

 I III V VI IX

InfoNation from the United Nations

http://cyberschoolbus.un.org/infonation3/menu/advanced.asp

InfoNation is an easy-to-use, two-step database that allows students and teachers to view and compare the most up-to-date statistical data for the member states of the United Nations. This is an excellent resource for student research or for inquiry lessons.

 I III V VI IX

Additional International Affairs and Organizations Websites

Electronic Embassy: A Resource of and for the Washington, D.C. Foreign Embassy Community
http://www.embassy.org

Embassy World: A Directory of All the World's Embassies and Consulates
http://www.embassyworld.com

Foreign Government Resources on the Web
http://www.lib.umich.edu/govdocs/foreign.html

Governments on the World Wide Web
http://www.gksoft.com/govt/en

Library of Congress Country Studies
http://lcweb2.loc.gov/frd/cs/cshome.html

Ministries of Foreign Affairs Online
http://www.le.ac.uk/dsp/mfas.html

North Atlantic Treaty Organization (NATO)
http://www.nato.int

Universal Currency Converter
http://www.xe.net/ucc/full.shtml

Virtual Sources of Maps and Data
http://www.virtualsources.com

Citizenship Education and Political Science

Full participation in a democratic society calls for informed participation in government, thoughtful voting, and insightful monitoring of government activity. The resources in this chapter help teachers foster those skills and attitudes among their students.

CIVIC IDEALS AND PRACTICES

Being a good citizen means participating knowledgeably in community and government affairs at all levels. These sites help teachers foster civic participation by individual students and entire classes.

Center for Civic Education

http://www.civiced.org

The Center for Civic Education is a nonprofit, nonpartisan educational corporation dedicated to fostering informed, responsible participation in civic life by citizens committed to democratic values and principles. Its easy-to-navigate site provides curricular materials, Internet links and resources, and articles and papers on civic education and responsible citizenship.

 V VI X

CivNet

http://www.civnet.org

At the heart of this site, sponsored by CIVITAS, an international organization devoted to civic education, is a monthly journal of articles about the state of democracy and civic education. Its civic education resource library features online links to lessons plans, syllabi, historical documents, journals, newsletters, and other materials. Civics teachers should bookmark this site.

 V VI X

Youth Activism Project

http://www.youthactivism.com/content.php?ID=6

Youth Activism seeks to engage young people under the age of 18, "the 26% solution," in solving problems in their communities and our nation. Billed as a "Democracy Dropout Prevention Clearinghouse," this site provides help and information to parents, mentors, teachers, principals, policymakers, and other adult allies who want to collaborate with youth to achieve positive community change.

 V VI X

The Educator's Reference Desk: Civics

http://www.eduref.org

From the Information Institute of Syracuse, the people who created AskEric, the Gateway to Educational Materials, the Virtual Reference Desk, and the Educator's Reference Desk, this site brings more than 2,000 lesson plans, 3,000 links to online education sources, and a question archive of specific information for teachers and students. This is an especially rich resource for social studies teachers. From the main page, go to "Subjects," then "Civics."

 I II III V VI VII IX X

American Promise

http://www.farmers.com/FarmComm/AmericanPromise/

Based on the popular KQED and PBS series, American Promise is a program from Farmers' Insurance that brings government to life by engaging students in the political process in their own classrooms. Themes include Touchstones of Our Society, The Challenges We Face, Acting on These Ideas, and Keeping the Promise.

 V VI X

Additional Civic Ideals and Practices Websites

Closeup Foundation Online
http://www.closeup.org

Presidential Classroom Homepage
http://www.presidentialclassroom.org

POLITICAL SCIENCE

The central obligation of responsible citizenship is informed voting in local, state, and national elections. These sites focus on the political process and provide help for educators in teaching students about this critical form of participation in a democratic society.

Federal Election Commission; http://www.fec.gov

Federal Election Commission

http://www.fec.gov

In 1975, Congress created the Federal Election Commission (FEC) to administer and enforce the Federal Election Campaign Act (FECA)—the statute that governs the financing of federal elections. The duties of the FEC, which is an independent regulatory agency, are to disclose campaign finance information, to enforce the provisions of the law such as the limits and prohibitions on contributions, and to oversee the public funding of presidential elections. This site provides detailed reports on individual, corporate, and PAC contributions to candidates and incumbents.

 V VI X

Project Vote Smart

http://www.vote-smart.org

Vote Smart tracks the performance of more than 13,000 government officials at the national, state, and local levels. It also provides engaging educational activities and teacher lessons that focus on how citizens can improve their representation in government affairs.

 V VI X

League of Women Voters

http://www.lwv.org

The League of Women Voters encourages informed, active participation by citizens in government, promotes understanding of public policy issues, and influences policy through public education and advocacy. The league provides its own materials on how to get involved, as well as links to many other voter education sites.

 V VI X

Politics and Government Resources

http://education.indiana.edu/~socialst

Hosted by Indiana University, this resource guide is part of a much more comprehensive gateway for social studies educators and students. It provides links to major political organizations, as well as nonpartisan groups and political science scholars throughout the nation.

 V VI X

Rock the Vote

http://www.rockthevote.org

Founded by members of the recording industry to fight censorship, Rock the Vote is "dedicated to protecting freedom of expression and to helping young people realize and utilize their power to effect change in the civic and political lives of their communities." Much of this organization's focus is upon changing voter registration procedures to encourage greater participation by young people. It also provides guidance on how to influence the political process in local communities.

 V VI X

Teaching Politics: Techniques and Technologies

http://teachpol.tcnj.edu

Produced by Professor William Ball at the College of New Jersey, this site is dedicated to providing images of political history, including famous persons, events, and challenges to American democracy. More than 500 photos exist in a searchable archive.

 V VI X

Center for American Women and Politics

http://www.rci.rutgers.edu/~cawp

A program of the Eagleton Institute at Rutgers University, the center provides fact sheets on women in elected offices from Congress through state legislatures. It also provides information on women as candidates and historical information on the role of women in the political process in America.

V VI X

Open Secrets: The Center for Responsive Politics

http://www.opensecrets.org

Open Secrets is an online source for data about money in politics. This site shows how money flows into political campaigns and provides analyses of who is contributing to whom and for what purposes. This is an interesting site for both teacher and student research.

 V VI X

British Broadcasting Corporation World Service (BBC)

http://www.bbc.co.uk/worldservice/index.shtml

Often, the most interesting perspective on one's own country comes from abroad. The BBC World Service home page provides news from the United States (and almost everywhere else) in English. It also provides a guide to local BBC programming in the United States.

 V VI IX X

ADVOCACY AND POLITICAL ACTION GROUPS

The expansion of the Internet has spawned a number of grassroots political organizations that can mobilize their members to lobby Congress for specific agendas. Two of the largest such organizations are Move On and True Majority. While controversial, their influence on the American political landscape is growing and promises to shape future public debate and elections.

 V VI X

Move On
http://www.moveon.org

True Majority
http://www.truemajority.org

POLITICAL PARTIES

Although clearly reflecting their own positions and agendas, political party websites provide good samples of party platforms, campaign strategies, and unique stances on important issues.

 V VI X

Democratic National Committee
http://www.democrats.org

Reform Party
http://www.reformparty.org

Republican National Committee
http://www.rnc.org

NEWS MEDIA

Massive coverage of political campaigns, congressional and legislative actions, and court decisions is provided on virtually all television and radio news shows, in newspapers, and in news magazines. The websites maintained by these organizations give up-to-the-minute reporting on critical issues in government.

Be sure to check out the websites for your local news media and add them to this list.

 V VI X

Television Sources

Colorful, highly interactive, and updated from minute to minute, these websites are good places to begin student coverage of important campaigns.

ABC News
http://abcnews.go.com/Politics/

CBS News
http://www.cbsnews.com/politics

CNN Interactive
http://www.cnn.com/ALLPOLITICS

C-Span
http://www.c-span.org

MSNBC
http://www.msnbc.com/news/politics_front.asp

Newspapers

Hundreds of newspapers cover thousands of local political stories every day. These four are noted for their national and international political coverage.

Chicago Tribune
http://www.chicagotribune.com

Los Angeles Times
http://www.latimes.com/news/politics

New York Times
http://www.nytimes.com/pages/politics/index.html

Washington Post
http://www.washingtonpost.com/wp-dyn/politics

Weekly News Magazines

News magazines provide feature stories on current political events, often going behind the scenes for in-depth coverage and analysis. The three largest news weeklies maintain excellent websites with dozens of useful features.

Newsweek
http://www.newsweek.com

Time
http://www.pathfinder.com/time

U.S. News and World Report
http://www.usnews.com/usnews/home.htm

Geography

In October 1994, the U.S. National Geography Standards were published in Washington, D.C. An extensive presentation of these 18 standards with lesson plans and activities is available from the National Geographic Society's website **Xpeditions**.

Xpeditions—NGS

http://www.nationalgeographic.com/xpeditions/standards/index.html

This site should be the starting point for teachers who will teach geography. There are lesson plans sorted by grade level, activities, a multiview atlas, and other resources tied to the national geography standards.

 I III IX

National Geographic Society

http://www.nationalgeographic.com

This is a gateway website that provides access to the world of geography. Xpeditions provides more than 600 printable maps for use in the classroom and a variety of activities and information that would enhance geography education. It regularly offers special features on its Expeditions and Exhibits sections.

 I III IV

National Council for Geographic Education

http://www.ncge.org

In addition to council events and programs, under "Activities" one can progress through a tutorial that explains the approaches and ideas for the Six Geography

Themes and Eighteen Standards of Geography. This site is particularly valuable for a teacher unfamiliar with the standards.

 I III IX

Reprinted with permission of the United States Geological Survey.

United States Geological Survey

http://mapping.usgs.gov/

This site offers detailed information, activities, and lesson plans that cover the broad spectrum of physical geography. It includes science-related topics such as U.S. natural resources, natural hazards, geospatial data, oceanography, climate, atmosphere, and so on, and issues that affect our quality of life. You should visit the Educational Resources and Science Topics resources.

 I III IX

National Atlas of the United States

http://www.nationalatlas.gov

This site, also developed by the U.S. Geological Survey, creates an atlas of U.S. natural and social-cultural landscapes. Interactive multimedia maps aid in the visualization and comprehension of complex relationships among places, people, and environments. You will need to download the Shockwave plug-in, which is provided by the site.

 I III IX

Google Earth

http://earth.google.com/

At this site you can download the software and desktop icon for Google Earth. This interactive, satellite-based view of the earth can be used to view the world from space and, with the zoom features, the roof of your house or any home in the world.

 III IX

About.com—Geography

http://geography.about.com/library/maps/blindex.htm#d

At About.com, you can download blank and completed maps for use in the classroom. This site also serves as a gateway to other sites with collections of maps and resources.

 I III IX

CIA Factbook

http://www.odci.gov/cia/publications/factbook/index.html

An up-to-date and factually accurate listing of data by country that is updated in real time. Includes categories such as maps, transportation, people, government, economy, communications, and transnational issues.

I III IX

50 States and Capitals

http://www.50states.com

This site provides easy access to statistical and historical information for each of the 50 states of the union. Also included are the lyrics to state songs; the melodies can be heard with Real Player software.

 III

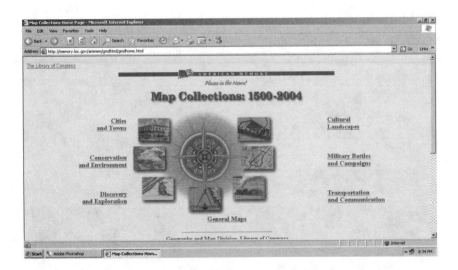

Library of Congress American Memory Historical Collection

http://memory.loc.gov/ammem/gmdhtml/gmdhome.html

An array of historical and contemporary maps of North America can be accessed and used in history and geography classes.

 II III

Historical Maps at the University of Texas Library

http://www.lib.utexas.edu/maps/historical/index.html

This site has original resources, as well as links to other sites with historical maps organized by periods and regions. This resource can be used for history or geography.

 II III IX

Explore the Globe Program

http://www.globe.gov/fsl/welcome.html

This site is ideal for elementary-level teachers who have a strong interest in active learning approaches. In addition to interactive activities for students, educators can access a teacher's guide, a data archive, and an image gallery.

 I III IV

Leonard's "Cam World"

http://www.leonardsworlds.com/camera.html

This travel-based site offers more than 2,500 outdoor cameras in real time at locations around the world. Visitors can access travel information for cities and other locations.

I III IV

Reprinted with permission of Richard Darsie.

Tales of Wonder

http://www.darsie.net/talesofwonder/

This is an excellent site for integration of literature into social studies geography curricula.

 I II IX

The Global Schoolhouse

http://www.gsn.org

This site provides advice on use of the Internet to connect with schools around the world. It offers many projects that encourage global awareness.

 III IX

The Great Globe Gallery

http://www.staff.amu.edu.pl/~zbzw/glob/glob1.htm

This site has hundreds of images of the globe and information on global changes.

 III IX

Additional Geography Websites

Awesome Library
http://www.awesomelibrary.org/Library/Materials_Search/Lesson_Plans/Social_Studies.html

Blank Maps of Countries and States
http://geography.about.com/cs/blankoutlinemaps/

E-conflict World Encyclopedia
http://www.emulateme.com

Ellis Island Virtual Tour
http://teacher.scholastic.com/activities/immigration/tour/

Epals Classroom Exchange
http://www.epals.com/home.html

ETHNOLOGUE: Languages of the World
http://www.sil.org/ethnologue

Flags of the World
http://atlasgeo.span.ch/fotw/flags/iso3166.html

Florida Alliance's 100 Geography Lesson Plans
http://fga.freac.fsu.edu/lessonplans.html

Gateway to Geography Games
http://members.aol.com/bowermanb/games.html

Geography and Economics Lesson Plans for 32 Children's Books
http://www.mcps.k12.md.us/curriculum/socialstd/Econ_Geog.html

Geography Time Line and Encyclopedia
http://www.ucmp.berkeley.edu/help/timeform.html

GIS Dictionary of Geography Terms
http://www.geo.ed.ac.uk/agidict/welcome.html

Maps of Native American Nations
http://www.kstrom.net/isk/maps/mapmenu.htmlPhsycial

National Geographic's Map Matching
http://www.nationalgeographic.com/maps/

National Weather Service
http://www.nws.noaa.gov

The Population Reference Bureau
http://www.prb.org/template.cfm?Section=LessonPlans&Template=/
LessonPlans.cfm

A Solar/Terrestrial Tutorial
http://vortex.plymouth.edu/sun.html

U.S. Census Bureau Data 1790–1960
http://fisher.lib.virginia.edu/census/

The University of South Florida Geography Webquest
http://www.coedu.usf.edu/main/departments/seced/
GeographyWebQuest.htm

The Weather Channel
http://www.weather.com/

Yale University Map Collection
http://www.library.yale.edu/MapColl/curious.html

Economics

No aspect of the social studies touches our lives more directly than economics. Virtually every decision we make every day is affected in some way by economic forces. Fortunately, there are excellent resources for teachers who wish to incorporate this critical and engaging subject into their classes. Most of the websites featured in this section include lesson plans and instructional materials for K–12 use. Others provide research data, interactive experiences for students, or online access to programs and projects sponsored by governments, educational institutions, businesses, or other agencies.

The Department of the Treasury; http://www.treas.gov/kids/

U.S. Treasury Department

http://www.treas.gov/education

Treasury's home page tells the story of the department with an illustrated history beginning with its founding in 1789. The link to the Bureau of Engraving and Printing website offers educational games, teacher resources, and a chat room where students can ask questions about money and how it is produced.

 II V VI VII X

The United States Mint; http://www.usmint.gov/

U.S. Mint

http://www.usmint.gov

This government site provides excellent information on how money is actually made, entered into circulation, and, eventually, collected and destroyed. Especially interesting is the section on counterfeiting and fraud. A slick set of "flash" presentations, called "The Time Machine" and "Hip Pocket Change," present engaging information on the links between money and historical events.

 II V VI VII

National Council on Economic Education

http://www.nationalcouncil.org

The National Council on Economic Education is a partnership of leaders in education, business, and labor devoted to helping youngsters function in a changing global economy. This is an especially rich source of information, teaching materials, and teacher training opportunities. The council also sponsors Economics America, a network of state councils and more than 260 university-based centers for economic education. This site is a gateway to lessons, content materials, and other valuable websites devoted to the teaching of economics and sound economic decision making by students at all levels of education. Among the many engaging resources are economic simulations, materials for students in grades K–12, and planning tools for teachers. The EconEdLink® section makes it easy for teachers to access websites that support economics curricula. It includes hundreds of lesson plans for K–12 teachers and serves as a portal for dozens of other engaging and useful sites.

 VII IX

Economic Education Web

http://ecedweb.unomaha.edu/home.htm

The Economic Education Web, or EcEdWeb, is sponsored by the University of Nebraska at Omaha's Center for Economic Education. This award-winning site offers comprehensive resources for teachers at all levels (K–college). Besides serving as a superb gateway to other economics education sites, EcEdWeb provides excellent materials of its own, including key economic concepts for students at all levels, descriptions of "evidence of student learning" that can be used to shape assessments, and thoughtful suggestions on using the Internet to teach economics concepts in K–12 school settings. The links to other websites have been selected and reviewed for both quality of content and ease of use. This is an excellent place to start for teachers developing an economics curriculum in their own schools or for those who want to integrate economics content into other subject fields. Activities are linked to Nebraska standards, which are similar to those of many other states.

 VII IX

NetEc

http://netec.wustl.edu/NetEc.html

Hosted by Washington University's Department of Economics, NetEc is an international academic effort to improve the communication of economics via electronic media. Although it is not currently being updated, two of its most useful subsections continue to be WebEc, a hosted, searchable library of free economics resources on the Internet, and JokeEc, a vast collection of jokes about economics that serve as an excellent springboard for the teaching of basic economic concepts as well as some of its more subtle nuances. This award-winning site is a great source of background information for teachers who are interested in enriching their own understanding of economics and econometrics as well.

 VII IX

Federal Reserve Bank of San Francisco

http://www.frbsf.org/education/index.html

The Federal Reserve Bank is the central bank of the United States. The San Francisco branch provides teaching resources on its own site, as well as links to other economics education sites across the Internet. The site supplies both student materials and lesson plans focusing on the history and development of monetary systems, simulations exploring supply and demand, an economics treasure hunt, and an "Ask Dr. Econ" feature, where students can get responses to specific questions about money and economics.

 VII IX

The Mint

http://www.themint.org

The Mint, which bills itself as an integrated website for middle school and high school students, their teachers, and their parents, is provided by Northwestern Mutual Life Insurance and the National Council on Economic Education. Focused on the individual and the economy, this site provides information on starting your own business, saving and investing, spending and consuming, budgeting, and your role in the economy. Special features include tools that help students analyze their earning, saving, and spending habits and straightforward information about investing tailored for young people. This is an excellent site for both information and engaging activities.

 VI IX

The World Bank

http://www.worldbank.org/html/schools

Recently surrounded by controversy, the World Bank is a global effort to invest in those nations where the need is greatest. In addition to materials on the teaching of economics, the World Bank website provides information on developing countries and regions, the big issues in the developing world, and solid economic data that can be used for research and instruction. Its stated mission to help cultivate empathy and respect for people in developing nations leads this site to help students experience poverty and the promise of economic growth through the eyes of children and adults in these nations.

 VII IX

The Stock Market Game

http://www.smg2000.org

The Stock Market Game was the first—and is still one of the best—large-scale simulations about how money and investing work to power a global economy. Over the course of 10 weeks, participants invest their hypothetical $100,000 in NASDAQ, AMEX, and NYSE stocks. They research stocks, study how the financial markets work, choose their portfolios, manage budgets, follow companies in the news, and make decisions on whether to buy, sell, or hold. They can compare their portfolios' performance to those of peers on a weekly basis. The Stock Market Game is a trademark of the Foundation for Investor Education, a nonprofit organization dedicated to developing and providing learning resources for investors of all ages, raising the level of investor awareness in the United States, supporting research programs, and advocating the advancement of investor education.

 VII IX

EconoLink from the Progress Report

http://www.progress.org/econolink

This gateway site is sponsored by the Progress Report, part of the Economic Justice Network. The site offers links to a number of interesting and provocative resources, many of which provide a view of economic behavior and policy that is quite different from capitalism and market economics. Students, journalists, activists, and program developers can all find material that challenges conventional wisdom and provides counterpoint to mainstream economic education sites.

 VII IX X

Consumer Information Center

http://www.pueblo.gsa.gov

Provided by the Consumer Information Center of the U.S. General Services Administration (GSA), this site gives access to hundreds of product information resources and consumer guides on everything from buying a car to looking for a job. This is an excellent site for students engaged in research on popular products and informed buying.

 VII

U.S. Department of Commerce

http://www.commerce.gov

The Commerce Department is charged with promoting job growth, sustainable development, and improved economic opportunities for all citizens. Through the National Oceanic and Atmospheric Administration, it makes possible the weather reports heard every morning; it facilitates technology that Americans use in the workplace and at home every day; it supports the development, gathering, and transmitting of information essential to competitive business; it makes possible the diversity of companies and goods found in America's (and the world's) marketplaces; it supports environmental and economic health for the communities in which Americans live; and it conducts the constitutionally mandated decennial census, which is the basis of representative democracy. The department's website is a gateway to all these useful and informative resources, which support sound economics instruction.

 VI VII IX X

Educator's Reference Desk

http://www.eduref.org/cgi-bin/print.cgi/Resources/Subjects/
Social_Studies/Economics.html

This very useful, teacher-friendly site provides lessons for all aspects of social studies. The economics section is especially good for teachers in grades 4–12. The lessons are all developed by practitioners for practitioners, so they are straightforward and workable. Most include all necessary materials.

 VI VII IX X

Escape from Knab

http://www.escapefromknab.com/land.html

In order to purchase the $10,000 ticket required to return to Earth, students must make good earning, investing, and savings decisions after finding themselves stranded on the planet Knab. Knabians are friendly enough, but slimy and foul-smelling. Naturally, kids love them—and this engaging game.

 VII IX

Lemonade Stand

http://www.lemonadegame.com

This is a World Wide Web version of the classic computer game Lemonade Stand, with several differences. "High Game Scores" posted on the site allow students to compete with the best-performing kids from all over the nation.

 VII

UBUYACAR

http://www.mcli.dist.maricopa.edu/pbl/ubuystudent/index.html

This problem-based learning site from Maricopa (Arizona) Community College leads students through a productive problem-solving process on how to make good economic decisions, specifically, how to buy a car. This is a real hit with middle and high school kids.

 VII

New York Stock Exchange

http://www.nyse.com/about/education/1098034584990.html

The NYSE's education section offers teaching materials, as well as high-quality, nontechnical information about the world's largest stock exchange and how it functions. This is a great site for older students.

 VII

AFL-CIO

http://www.aflcio.org/home.htm

Representing more than 13 million workers, the nation's largest labor union provides useful information on the history of the labor movement and a labor perspective on contemporary issues and the global economy.

 II V VII IX X

Stat-USA

http://www.stat-usa.gov/

This site provides thousands of electronic data files, more than 700 of which are updated every day. These data cover dozens of topics, including economic indicators, employment, foreign trade, and more than 20 other subjects.

 VII IX

Young Investor

http://www.younginvestor.com/

Young Investor, from Columbia Management, offers an excellent comprehensive site for kids, teachers, parents, and teens. It provides age-appropriate information on investing, as well as a number of tools and lessons for important savings and investment concepts.

 V VII X

Economics and Geography Lessons for 32 Children's Books

http://www.mcps.k12.md.us/curriculum/socialstd/Econ_Geog.html

This teacher-friendly site from the Montgomery (Maryland) County Public Schools provides lessons for teaching economics content through 32 different children's books. Written by teachers, this site is very practical and triggers ideas for developing economics lessons around other children's books and young adult books as well.

 III V VII X

Additional Economics Websites

Bureau of Labor Statistics
http://stats.bls.gov

Classroom Lessons from Ayers on Line
http://www.ayersonline.com/Toolbox/tool.htm

Current Value of Old Money
http://www.ex.ac.uk/~RDavies/arian/current/howmuch.html

Internal Revenue Service
http://www.irs.gov

Resources for Economists on the Internet
http://rfe.wustl.edu/EconFAQ.html

Tax Policy
http://www.taxpolicy.com

CHAPTER

9

Anthropology, Sociology, and Psychology

Sociology and anthropology are closely aligned disciplines that examine human interactions. Sociology is focused on group processes, and anthropology centers on cultural change and diffusion. Psychology focuses on humans' behavior and thoughts as humans interact with stimuli in the environment. A number of websites capture the far-ranging scope of these disciplines.

ANTHROPOLOGY AND SOCIOLOGY

Reprinted with permission of the American Anthropological Association.

American Anthropological Association

http://www.aaanet.org/

This is the official site of the American Anthropological Association (AAA), which provides access to brochures (e.g., "What Is Anthropology?"), as well as press releases on recent articles and papers published by the AAA. The site is broken down into several categories: careers, ethics, government affairs, minority issues in anthropology, press relations, publications, and anthropology resources on the Internet. This site is updated weekly and claims to be current on issues and concerns in the field of anthropology. There are more than 50 links on this site to other informative resources related to anthropology.

 I II IV V

Museum of Anthropology at the University of British Columbia

http://www.moa.ubc.ca/

Online exhibits on a variety of anthropological topics, as well as a virtual tour of the museum, are among the highlights of this website. A number of sourcebooks that focus on an area of cultural significance can be found in full text. A special section for K–12 school programs has links to websites and materials that can be used in the classroom.

 I III IV V IX

ArchNet

http://www.lib.uconn.edu/ArchNet

A well-organized, comprehensive site of anthropology that includes links to more than 119 museums, anthropology sites, and universities. This site excels in both its subject areas, ranging from archaeometry to method and theory sections, and regional search capabilities. This search feature can locate any place on the globe and give you a list of all sites pertaining to this geographic area. This site is easily translated into several languages, a helpful feature for bilingual students. Also included is a search engine by subject or area of interest, links to journals and other online publications, online site tours, and software for mapping.

 I II III IV

Anthropology Resources at the University of Kent

http://lucy.ukc.ac.uk/

This is a truly unique site that allows people to witness what anthropological fieldwork is like. The site features Stephon Lyon, a doctoral student from the University of Kent, who is doing research in Bhaloti, a village in northern Pakistan. Visitors to this website can read Lyon's daily field notes, as well as weekly updates and monthly reports. In addition, visitors can read stories and listen to music created by the villagers themselves. Lyon encourages people to send him comments about his research.

 I II IV V IX X

Smithsonian Institution Libraries, Anthropology on the Internet for K–12

http://www.sil.si.edu/SILPublications/Anthropology-K12

This site gives its visitors a broad review of anthropology with historical and current issues and research. Specific topics on the site include, but are not limited to, archaeology, social/cultural anthropology, physical anthropology, and linguistics. There is a comprehensive Internet guide to resources about many different cultures—past and present—ranging from excavations and site/regional reports to concept and teaching sites. The site gives access to virtual exhibits, electronic publications, and career links. In addition, there are numerous illustrations and pictures of artifacts.

I II III IV V IX X

The Peace Corps.

Peace Corps Global Education World Wise Schools

http://www.peacecorps.gov/wws/guides/looking/index.html

The goal of the site "Looking at Ourselves and Others" is to challenge "World Wise" students to become more conscious of the values they share with their families, friends, and communities. The site provides analytical tools that help combat stereotypical thinking and enhance cross-cultural communication. The teacher's guide is arranged by topic, including teacher background information, activity outlines, and student worksheets. Many activities are similar to those used to help prepare Peace Corps volunteers for their cross-cultural experiences. The activities for each topic are further divided according to three suggested groupings: grades 3–5, 6–9, and 10–12. Each activity outline has at least six parts: an estimate of class time needed, materials, a statement of objectives, step-by-step procedures, debriefing exercises, and suggestions for extending the activity.

 I III IV V VI VII IX X

Roadsideamerica.com

http://www.roadsideamerica.com/

This is an excellent site in which the viewer is able to see many of America's strangest roadside attractions, unknown to many. The slogan of the site sums it up very well: "Your on-line guide to offbeat attractions." At this site, you are able to view the odd attractions in a state of your choice or follow a road trip, set up by the experts at this site, to see many of these great attractions.

 I IV V

Florida's Underwater Archaeological Preserves

http://dhr.dos.state.fl.us/archaeology/underwater/preserves/

This is a wonderful site that explores and discusses Florida's statewide system of underwater parks featuring shipwrecks and other historical underwater sites. This site includes pictures and descriptions of the nine current parks, as well as others that are under development. Each archaeological site is open year-round and free of charge.

 II IV

American Museum of Natural History

http://www.amnh.org/

This interactive site provides visitors with detailed information on natural history. Time lines provide specific information on periods dating back to the Devonian period and up to the Pleistocene period. Visitors to this site can also take a tour through numerous exhibitions in the museum, including one of the world's largest exhibits of dinosaur fossils. While visiting this site, one can also look up current events or witness a volcano erupt.

 I II III IV IX

The University of Memphis Institute of Egyptian Art and Archaeology

http://academic.memphis.edu/egypt//main.html

This website is dedicated to ancient Egypt. Teachers and students can take a tour of different places in Egypt and see color photos of various attractions. For example, a student or teacher can take a tour of Giza and see photos of the pyramids and the Sphinx. Visitors can see photos of different Egyptian artifacts as well. The site also has links to other Egyptian websites, including one where teachers and students can learn about the different gods and their stories and myths. There is also a link to a site where students can learn about Egypt today.

 I II III

Reprinted with permission of the Gallup Organization.

The Gallup Organization

http://www.gallup.com/

The Gallup Organization website deals with current events. There are also articles about politics and current social issues affecting our society. Teachers and students can use this site to learn about current events, people's reactions to them, and issues affecting our world today.

 I III IV V VII VIII IX X

Additional Anthropology and Sociology Websites

Allyn and Bacon Sociology
http://www.abacon.com/sociology/soclinks/index.html

American Sociological Association
http://www.asanet.org/index.ww

Anthropology Fieldstudy: The Anthropologist in the Field
http://www.melanesia.org/fieldwork/tamakoshil/

Anthropology in the News
http://www.tamu.edu/anthropology/news.html

Archaeological Institute of America
http://www.archaeological.org/

The Archaeology Channel
http://www.archaeologychannel.org/

Critical Bibliography on North American Indians
http://www.nmnh.si.edu/anthro/outreach/Indbibl/index.html

Cultural Survival
http://209.200.101.189/

Department of Anthropology National Museum of Natural History
http://www.nmnh.si.edu/anthro/outreach/outrch1.html

Dig: The Archaeology Magazine for Kids
http://www.digonsite.com/

Erasing Native American Stereotypes
http://www.nmnh.si.edu/anthro/outreach/sterotyp.html

Kinship and Social Organization
http://www.umanitoba.ca/anthropology/kintitle.html

Library of Congress American Folklife Center
http://lcweb.loc.gov/folklife/

LSU Libraries—Anthropology Subject Guide
http://www.lib.lsu.edu/soc/anthro.html

MadSci Network Anthropology
http://www.madsci.org

MayaQuest
http://www.teachervision.fen.com/tv/classroomconnect/maya/

Nacirema
http://www.beadsland.com/nacirema

National Association for Humane and Environmental Education
http://www.nahee.org/

Native Web
http://www.nativeweb.org

oldstoneage.com
http://www.oldstoneage.com/

Oriental Institute
http://www-oi.uchicago.edu/OI/default.html

Rabbit in the Moon
http://www.halfmoon.org/

The Simon Fraser University Museum of Archaeology and Ethnology
http://www.sfu.ca/archaeology/museum/

A Sociological Tour Through Cyberspace
http://www.trinity.edu/~mkearl/

The SocioSite Project Social and Cultural Anthropology
http://www2.fmg.uva.nl/sociosite/topics/anthropo.html

The SocioSite Project Sociological Theories and Perspectives
http://www2.fmg.uva.nl/sociosite/topics/theory.html

Stone Pages
http://www.stonepages.com/

Texas A&M Department of Anthropology Links
http://anthropology.tamu.edu/anthro_link.htm

University of Michigan Museum of Anthropology
http://www.lsa.umich.edu/umma/

The University of Pennsylvania Museum of Archaeology and Anthropology
http://www.museum.upenn.edu/

World Health Organization
http://www.who.int/home-page/

World Wide Email Directory of Anthropologists
http://wings.buffalo.edu/WEDA

PSYCHOLOGY

The most "human" of all the social sciences, psychology is all about people, as individuals, in groups, and as a species with very unique characteristics and abilities. Students are usually fascinated by the study of psychology, largely because it has built-in relevance to their own lives. The sites described here are important gateways to this vast and engaging field.

The American Psychological Society Teaching Resources

http://psych.hanover.edu/aps/teaching.html

The American Psychological Society provides a gateway to dozens of useful sites and resources specifically for the teaching of psychology. It includes materials for general, behavioral, cognitive, health, forensic, and social psychology, as well as information on statistics, research methods, and other topics related to the field. This site is straightforward and helpful for teachers and more mature students.

 III IV V

Discovering Psychology

http://www.learner.org/discoveringpsychology/index.html

This is the companion website to the video series and telecourse with Philip G. Zimbardo, Ph.D. The site includes interactive sections on the human brain, life span development, history of psychology, research methods, and approaches in practice. It also includes a glossary of psychology, information on pioneers in the field, and detailed text on all 26 programs in the series.

 I IV V

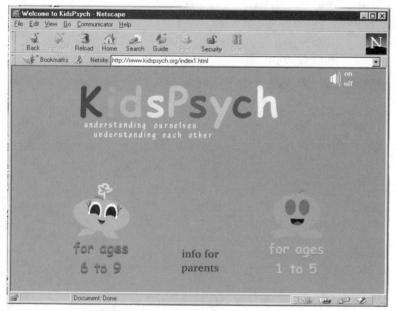

Reprinted with the permission of the American Psychological Association.

American Psychological Association—for Kids

http://www.kidspsych.org/index1.html

Provided by the APA, this engaging site is all about "understanding ourselves and understanding each other." It includes entertaining games that challenge children to think in new and creative ways. For each activity, the site provides a list of theoretical and research publications that address the psychology of the task. Forget about the kids; adults will spend hours on this one.

 IV V

American Psychological Association

http://www.apa.org

The APA's site offers a "public" section that provides well-written materials on a number of contemporary psychological issues, such as mental health, applied behavior, or social problems. Designed for teachers of psychology in secondary schools, the TOPSS section of this site (http://www.apa.org/ed/topsshomepage.html) offers excellent resources for high school instructors and students. The help site (http://helping.apa.org) gives access to online assistance with real-life problems.

 III IV V

Office of Teaching Resources in Psychology

http://teachpsych.lemoyne.edu/teachpsych/div/teachpsychlinks.html

This site provides teachers with access to instructional materials in psychology and related fields. Sponsored by the Society for the Teaching of Psychology, it links directly to other specialist organizations, as well as to other gateway sites.

 IV V

The Gateway

http://www.thegateway.org/

The Gateway to Educational Materials (GEM) project is an effort to provide teachers with quick and easy access to vast, uncataloged collections of educational materials on various federal, state, university, nonprofit, and commercial Internet sites. To access the section on psychology, either type in "psychology" in the search field or click on "Browse Subjects" under "Search the Gateway," scroll to the social studies, and click on "psychology." The site is linked to some of the most important resources in the field and includes instructional units on conflict resolution, decision making, and generational conflicts, to name just a few.

 IV V

Classics in the History of Psychology

http://psychclassics.yorku.ca/

This fascinating resource was developed by Christopher Green from York University, Toronto, Canada. It provides full-text versions of the classics in the field, from the ancients to contemporary thinkers and scholars. This is a virtual textbook for a history-of-psychology course, and a great resource for students and teachers.

 IV V

Neuroscience for Kids

http://faculty.washington.edu/chudler/neurok.html

This highly interactive site leads students on an exploration of the nervous system. From playing synaptic tag to singing songs about the brain, teachers can access engaging activities, experiments, and new discoveries on this well-designed site.

 IV V

Additional Psychology Websites

American Psychological Association: National High School Psychology Standards
http://www.apa.org/ed/natlstandards.html

Pfizer Brain: The World Inside Your Head
http://www.pfizer.com/brain/etour1.html

The Society for the Teaching of Psychology
http://teachpsych.lemoyne.edu/

Teachers of Psychology in Secondary Schools (TOPSS)
http://www.apa.org/ed/topsshomepage.html

The World of Abnormal Psychology
http://www.learner.org/resources/series60.html

Teaching About Controversial Issues, Tolerance, and Equity

Social studies, more than any other subject taught in schools, requires the teacher to diplomatically engage students in discussions that deal with highly personal and controversial public issues. The range of controversial issues in social studies that might be part of a classroom experience is potentially infinite. Intolerance in the form of racism, sexism, classism, and discrimination rejects diversity and stifles equity. Conversely, when differences are celebrated for bringing richness to interactions, changes leading toward social justice can be initiated.

The following sites explore links that can foster tolerance and cooperation; they can be helpful not only for teachers and students but also for parents. However, the special challenge imposed on social studies teachers requires a robust understanding of issues and a willingness to forge and maintain a democratic classroom. The following resources provide background information and suggested teaching methods on a number of controversial topics.

Reprinted with permission of Public Agenda Online.

Public Agenda Online

http://www.publicagenda.org

This site is an up-to-date resource for information on a variety of topics from abortion to welfare. Each section contains an overview of the issue, fact files, ideas on how to frame the debate, unique statistics, graphs, and so on.

Controversial Issues—Multnomah Public Library

http://www.multcolib.org/homework/sochc.html

At this site, you can find a clickable listing created to meet the needs of Multnomah County middle and high school students researching current social issues from multiple perspectives. For each topic, there are links to papers and other websites organized by pro and con and legislation that may bear on the topic.

Professional Cartoon Index

http://cagle.slate.msn.com/teacher/

Cartoons are an excellent way to introduce a current event that may be controversial. As an accepted form of social commentary, they provide powerful visuals that aid in the comprehension of multiple perspectives. This site includes cartoons from close to 100 daily newspapers.

Teaching Tolerance

http://www.splcenter.org/

The Southern Poverty Law Center web page on teaching tolerance addresses the efforts being made to help teach tolerance in the classroom. Links attached to the site give helpful information and resources for teachers on teaching tolerance of all races and other issues facing young people today.

Fighting Hate Across the Nation

http://www.civilrights.org/

This website is filled with a vast amount of information regarding intolerance. Visitors are provided with a definition of hate, statutes, laws, and so on. Real stories of people who have been affected by hate crimes are also included. Students can use this website to write papers or get information and statistics on these ethical issues. The Anti-Hate Resource Center is linked with other websites such as Cyberwatch, HateWatch, and the Anti-Defamation League.

Human Rights Watch

http://www.hrw.org

This site maintains updated information from around the world on human rights abuses. It includes breaking news, background information, ongoing events, and commentaries on regional abuses.

The Hate Directory

http://www.bcpl.lib.md.us/~rfrankli/hatedir.htm

This site provides visitors with a comprehensive list of hate groups on the Internet. Teachers may also find it useful as a reference or as a historical document, as defunct hate websites are included with the list of active hate sites. In addition, this site provides a directory of links to other web pages that combat hate on the Internet, such as HateWatch, the Anti-Defamation League, and Cyberwatch.

HateWatch

http://www.hatewatch.org

This project provides a public forum for those interested in exchanging views on hate crimes and prejudice. The catalog of current web-based hate groups allows visitors to view the sites that are being used to proliferate hate. HateWatch provides current news on evolving hate issues and gives assistance to hate crime victims. This site also includes video presentations, a web-based radio show, and online interviews with those advocating and condemning hate crimes.

Reprinted with permission of the Anti-Defamation League.

Anti-Defamation League (ADL)

http://www.adl.org

The ADL site allows visitors to be informed about issues of prejudice and discrimination by providing news on international affairs, legislation, and domestic events. Special topics, such as the Nation of Islam, terrorism on the Internet, and school vouchers, are displayed with related commentaries and news updates. Teachers are provided with lesson plans, videos, and books on prejudice and communication among diverse groups. There are helpful ideas for celebrating holidays in a way that is democratic. This site also allows parents to find ideas and sources to support communication with their children on issues of hate crimes and discrimination.

UNICEF Voices of Youth

http://www.unicef.org/voy

UNICEF has organized this site into three general areas that address global issues on children's rights: the Meeting Place, the Learning Place, and the Teacher's

Place. The Meeting Place is where students can go to share ideas with others around the world on issues concerning human rights. The Learning Place provides students with activities, such as quizzes on current children's rights topics, online classrooms, and suggestions for starting youth groups. Some of the activities might focus on areas such as child labor, HIV/AIDS, or unequal cultural treatment of girls. The Teacher's Place is where teachers are able to discuss educational and global issues with other teachers, plus find lesson plans, assignments, and links to other discussion groups.

Amnesty International (AI)

http://www.amnesty.org.uk

Amnesty International has developed this site in order for visitors to become involved in and informed about global human rights. The library contains reports on international campaigns against oppressive governments that are violating the International Declaration of Human Rights. Teacher resources are available, with videos of different amnesty campaigns, software packages, bibliographies of useful publications, and lesson plans integrating human rights awareness. Students are given resources in order to take action with letter-writing campaigns, assemblies, starting a youth group, and individual action packs. AI also provides the most recent press releases, articles, and updates on individual cases that have been the focus of a particular campaign by students and/or members of Amnesty International.

American Civil Rights Review

http://www.americancivilrightsreview.com/

This site provides the most current news on racism, civil rights, hate crimes, and discrimination. Various sources and websites are available to provide the complete perspective of civil rights issues through sound bites, articles, and links. This site will add fire to any discussion by allowing visitors access to other websites that promote conspiracy theories, white rights, circus freak rights, international genocide, immigration issues, and many more.

United Nations CyberSchoolBus Human Rights in Action

http://www0.un.org/cyberschoolbus/humanrights/index.asp

This site was developed to help students gain a sense of themselves by taking action against human rights abuse. Students can understand the International Declaration of Human Rights through an interactive process that provides activities, discussion topics, terminology and text explanations, and Q-and-A sessions with experts on the declaration. Teachers are encouraged to put their students into action with various lesson plans and projects. In addition, students and teachers can share

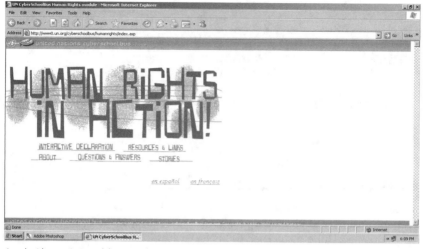

Reprinted with permission of the United Nations.

their ideas of action with others through online discussion groups. Other helpful links on this site educate visitors with a human rights bibliography, vocabulary builder, facts and figures, and personal stories of human rights abuses.

Distinguished Women of Past and Present

Reprinted with permission of Danuta Bois.

Distinguished Women of Past and Present

http://www.DistinguishedWomen.com

Visitors to this site can find biographical profiles of women of the past and present who have become distinguished in literature, education, science, politics, civil rights, art, entertainment, and other fields. Current updates of distinguished women in the news and the titles of recommended books written by or about women are also available on this site. Links to other web pages such as the Most Powerful Women in the World, Early Women Masters of the East and West, 100 Celebrated Chinese Women, and the Ecofeminism Homepage are included. The Black History Month feature allows a search by field for profiles of distinguished African American women and also provides helpful links to sites on African American history.

Women's Educational Equity Act (WEEA) Equity Resource Center

http://www.edc.org/WomensEquity

The Women's Educational Equity Act (WEEA) Equity Resource Center promotes awareness of gender equity among men and women in learning, developing, and achieving in society. Teachers can find lesson plans on gender equity legislation, sexual harassment issues, and distinguished women in history. WEEA Digest is available online to provide educators with current discussions on educational theory and field-based perspectives. There also are links to fun sites for girls, feminist sites, and online courses to engage middle school girls in math and science. E-mail discussions on equity issues are accessible, and information is provided for undergraduate women who want to become involved in gender equity issues on campus. Submission of gender equity materials, such as curricula or textbooks, to be evaluated by the WEEA expert panel, is encouraged.

Holocaust History Project

http://www.holocaust-history.org

This website provides educators as well as students interested in the Holocaust with free archives of documents and essays. Also included in this site are essays by and opinions of those who believe that the Holocaust never happened. Teachers will find the background information useful in sparking discussion of different viewpoints of the Holocaust, including those of racists. This site also allows visitors to ask questions on topics ranging from anti-Semitic influences to the children of the Holocaust. If the answer is not readily available, the site staff will find it for you. Also available at this site are recordings and photographs dating back to World War II.

Lest We Forget—The Untold History of America

http://www.coax.net/people/lwf/presentr.htm

A site dedicated to the accomplishments of African Americans, women, and Native Americans throughout the history of the United States. It contains a multitude of links, such as Writing Women into History, African Americans in the Revolutionary War Through the Vietnam War, Buffalo Soldiers, and Native

American History and Culture. The links emphasize that history can be viewed from various perspectives and that traditionally we have not received the full picture. The fact that these individuals' contributions have been overtly left out of textbooks is itself a lesson in racism and sexism.

Cybrary of the Holocaust

http://www.remember.org

This site contains many resources and educational activities in order that the memories of the Holocaust will not be forgotten by today's students. This cybrary provides teachers with various lesson plans ranging from topics on Jewish history to the Nazis' "Final Solution." Teachers may also meet other educators online through this site to share ideas, exchange lesson plans, and identify new books available on the topic. The images of the Holocaust are kept alive with a virtual tour of Auschwitz, various photo galleries, personal stories from survivors, and music that resulted from the events of World War II. This site also presents ways in which families of victims and survivors can find out the details and chronology of their family members' plight in the death camps. Students will be able to see art and poetry created by other students who have learned about the Holocaust.

Simon Wiesenthal Center

http://www.wiesenthal.com/

The Simon Wiesenthal Center web page is an interactive site that allows visitors to explore many different avenues, such as virtual exhibits, special collections, and teacher resources. The Wiesenthal Center deals with the effects of racism. The multimedia library allows users to examine different types of information. Links to sites that facilitate access to historical documents are also provided.

A Teacher's Guide to the Holocaust

http://fcit.coedu.usf.edu/holocaust/default.htm

This guide provides a wealth of information to teachers about the Holocaust. The site includes activities and resources for students and teachers. This Holocaust site provides a time line, as well as topics that describe people and the arts during this horrific time in history. Photographs and real-life stories of Jews are also displayed on this website.

Holocaust—Social Studies School Service

http://www.socialstudies.com/holo.html

This website provides many resources to support a social studies curriculum unit on the subject of the Holocaust. Teachers can find videos of contemporary films, CD-ROMs for Internet lessons, and many other media resources for the classroom. Samples from lesson plan books are provided to give educators some actual projects that are being used to present different perspectives. For example, projects are extracted from a unit plan based solely on the diaries of Anne Frank. Also helpful is a breakdown of what resources are appropriate for each grade level. Many links are provided, ranging from history tutorials to online museums.

WomenWatch

http://www.un.org./womenwatch

WomenWatch is a site dedicated to educating visitors on women's issues of advancement and empowerment. This site provides access to the global community of women who are working toward equity in areas of legislation, employment, and social status. Resources and links to women's organizations and conferences are provided in order to display the global organization of gender equity efforts. Statistical and comparative trends are also displayed in the areas of women's employment, literacy, education, and income. Updates on current news and events focusing on women's rights are also available, with links to other gender equity sites and resources.

Women's Internet Information Network

http://www.undelete.org

The Women's Internet Information Network contains more than 20,000 biographies of past and present accomplished women. In addition, this site has pictorial archives of photographs, prints, engravings, documents, and statues that exhibit the influence of women through different eras. Visitors to this site can also click on any day of the year to see what women accomplished on that day in history. The site contains links to organizations that fight for gender equity and provides a newsletter to present information on what is happening to women around the world.

Gender Issues: All One Heart, "Promoting Diversity Tolerance Through Education"

http://www.alloneheart.com

This is a positive and inspiring website for young adults and adults to explore. The site discusses issues regarding tolerance of all races and genders. One of the subject areas, Heart Burn, gives recent quotes by well-known people that include racially insensitive comments. This site also has an interactive message board to discuss hot topics and issues regarding discrimination without promoting religious "recruitments."

National Organization for Women (NOW)

http://www.now.org

NOW is the largest feminist organization in the United States, with more than 500,000 members. Through this website, users can learn about resources, legislation, and actions that are being taken to fight gender inequality. Some key issues that are discussed on this site include abortion, violence against women, and women in the military. Also located on the website is the NOW newsline, where members write up-to-date news articles regarding world trends and developments and how NOW relates to and is involved with these events.

Stop the Hate

http://www.stopthehate.org

This website is a student civil rights project that focuses on awareness and prevention of hate crimes. Teachers and students may find it useful as a resource in dealing with hate crimes and in deciding what hate crimes are taking place in their schools. The site also allows visitors to report hate crimes online and thus help victims locate local assistance.

African American History

http://historicaltextarchive.com/sections.php?op=listarticles&secid=8

This African American history site offers visitors a variety of topics and information regarding African Americans. The site allows people to view topics such as slavery, the military, and state and local history, as well as bibliographies that deal with African Americans. This site also provides information on African history in Canada. In addition, it provides visitors with several links, including the Black History Museum.

Crosspoint Anti-Racism

http://www.magenta.nl/crosspoint

This site is extremely useful for students, teachers, and parents alike. It gives more than a thousand different links to more than one hundred countries to view topics concerning antiracism. Users can select a country to view topics, or they can select a subject area such as "women," "human rights," or "Jewish resources." The site also gives direct connections to many search engines, which can be extremely helpful when searching topic areas online. There is also a place to share comments and ideas on antiracism.

Commission for Racial Equality

http://www.cre.gov.uk/index.html

This organization promotes equality in all facets of life. The site provides information on the law and how it affects people who fight against racism. It gives a complete background of the commission and its activities in the community. Information about discrimination and harassment is provided, as well as human rights involved in these issues. The commission also provides support in certain discrimination cases and resources for education.

Anger Management Workshop—For Teachers and Professionals

http://www.angermgmt.com/workshop.html

This site is great for teachers, administrators, and parents who want to learn strategies for coping with a child's anger. It offers a workshop on how to manage a child's anger and even your own. Recommended readings and ordering sources are provided. This site also includes a table of contents area that lists books, audiotapes, counseling, and a message board to answer any questions.

Beyond Prejudice

http://www.beyondprejudice.com/

Beyond Prejudice provides a multimedia guide on how to identify and change prejudice. This site provides materials that any teacher will find useful in the classroom, such as videotapes and printed material. The site is also an excellent way for administrators to train their staff on becoming aware of prejudice in their classrooms. A table of contents accompanies this site. Some of the areas that the table of contents highlights are a link to other related web pages, a quiz on prejudiced behavior, and a section on frequently asked questions.

Erasing Native American Stereotypes

http://www.nmnh.si.edu/anthro/outreach/sterotyp.html

Erasing Native American Stereotypes is located at the Smithsonian Institution's Anthropology Outreach Office website. This site offers teachers advice on how to accurately present and study American Indian cultures—an excellent and recommended starting point for teachers as they begin to create and prepare lessons.

Center for Democratic Renewal (CDR)

http://www.publiceye.org/

Originally known as the National Anti-Klan Network, the Center for Democratic Renewal (CDR) is a network of civil rights activists and organizations.

It was founded as a multiracial organization in 1979 in response to racist violence and Klan activity. Today the CDR works to promote its vision of a democratic and diverse society free of racism and bigotry. Through programs of research, public education, and community organizing, the CDR has expanded its vision to many communities across the country, helping to combat racism and all forms of bias.

Combating Racism and Intolerance

http://www.coe.int/t/E/human_rights/ecri/

This site provides visitors with a wide range of information. This list extends from international legal texts, to initiatives in education, to a listing of agencies that are currently active in the fight against racism. For teachers, there are videos and graphics that can be used in lesson plans dealing with racism and intolerance. This site also allows both teachers and students to exchange information while critiquing and commenting on fellow users' ideas. The site not only gives useful information on racism and intolerance but also shares examples of current ways of approaching racial problems.

International Education and Resource Network

http://www.iearn.org

Can we live in peace and coexistence with the rest of the world? This site provides an interactive tool to teach children from elementary to high school. There are various projects, such as folk games, global art and music, and laws of life, that students can tackle with the interaction of other classrooms around the world. The end result is that they find out that we are more alike than different from others and that young people can contribute to the good of our planet.

American Professional Society on the Abuse of Children (APSAC)

http://www.apsac.org

This group is dedicated to training the professionals who deal with child abuse. It offers a variety of resources, including training sessions. Users can access the guidelines and publications generated by this group, including the handbook created by APSAC. The site also lists the legislation that the group currently advocates. Users also have the option of joining this organization.

Prevent Child Abuse America (PCAA)

http://www.childabuse.org

The PCAA site provides information about the organization and its mission. In addition, the site lists resources for children, including hotline numbers and articles, such as "When Parents Drink Too Much." Also available are resources and information for parents. In addition to the resources generated by this organization, other resources, information, and links are available to users. Publications by the PCAA are available, and an opportunity to join this group is provided.

Religious Tolerance

http://www.religioustolerance.org/

This site describes both the positive and the negative aspects of religions. It describes dozens of faith groups, from Asatru to Christianity to Wicca to Zoroastrianism. Coverage includes new religious movements, cults, and belief systems, such as agnosticism, atheism, and humanism. The site describes all sides of each controversial topic, including abortion, physician-assisted suicide, capital punishment, evolution and creation science, and homosexuality.

Additional Tolerance Websites

ABA Dialogue on Freedom
http://www.dialogueonfreedom.org

ABC News
http://abcnews.go.com/

American-Arab Anti-Discrimination Committee (ADC)
http://www.adc.org

BBC News
http://news.bbc.co.uk/

CBS News
http://www.cbsnews.com

CNN
http://www.cnn.com

Controversy Education in Secondary Social Science Classrooms: Issues, Concerns, and Implementation
http://www.findarticles.com/p/articles/mi_qa4033/is_200310/ai_n9305417

Council on American Islamic Relations (CAIR)
http://www.cair-net.org

Council on Islamic Education
http://www.cie.org

Educators for Social Responsibility
http://www.esrnational.org/

ERIC Digest: Controversial Issues in the Classroom
http://www.ericdigests.org/pre-9218/issues.htm

FOX News
http://www.foxnews.com/

NBC News
http://www.nbc.com/News_&_Sports/

Network for Good
http://www.networkforgood.org/

PBS
http://www.pbs.org/

Teaching in a Pluralistic Society

Schools reflect society and attempt to provide all members of the American community an opportunity to succeed. Mainstreaming, latchkey children, immigration, economic differences, and technological changes present new challenges to teachers. The following resources will assist teachers in their attempts to teach all the students found in a contemporary school setting.

LEARNING STYLES AND MULTIPLE INTELLIGENCES

It has long been recognized that students have different ways of learning, and they often have a preferred mode of learning that is more developed than alternative forms. Moreover, students may differ in their preferences for learning environments or conditions. In order to meet the variety of instructional needs of students, multiple intelligences (MI) theory has focused on teaching using diverse lessons that call on many types of intelligence. The following sites expand on strategies for addressing multiple intelligence theory and learning styles in order to increase the success of more students in the classroom.

Multiple Intelligences and Learning Styles

http://pdonline.ascd.org/pd_demo/table_c.cfm?SID=24

This online course introduces students to the theory of multiple intelligences. The site includes interactive lessons that have been specially designed for Web-based training. Each lesson is supplemented with extensive reading material and access to discussion groups. This site also provides a stepping-stone for more in-depth study on the effects that different learning styles have on the classroom setting.

"I Think . . . Therefore . . . M.I.!"

http://surfaquarium.com/MI/

This website contains many links that exercise multiple intelligences. The site's creator has collected several viewpoints on Dr. Howard Gardner's theory of multiple intelligences, one of which is a candid interview with Gardner. There also are links to great thinkers and visionaries, including Mother Teresa, Albert Einstein, and Mark Twain.

Teaching to the Seven Multiple Intelligences

http://www.mitest.com/

This website provides a definition of multiple intelligences. It also presents an overview of research with accompanying graphics. Multiple intelligences information is broken down into age-groups, and tests are included for adults, youth, and children. This site also presents lesson plans to use in mathematics, social science, social studies, and art units. At the end of the website, there are links to other sites for multiple intelligences.

Education World

http://www.education-world.com/a_curr/curr054.shtml

This website defines multiple intelligence and the eight different kinds of intelligences discussed in *Frames of Minds* by Howard Gardner. Suggestions for implementing Gardner's theory in the classroom are described. Education World also has a section guide that enables the visitor to view other subjects, including science, special education, and parent issues. Teachers are provided lesson ideas and books that can be used in education.

Multiple Intelligence

http://www.ez2bsaved.com/Multiple_Intelligences/index-mi.htm

This site offers a comprehensive listing of links to sites on multiple intelligences with background information and teaching strategies. Moreover, an index is provided that includes articles, checklists, and tests that are available online.

Family Education Network: Learning Styles

http://www.familyeducation.com

This site provides visitors with a definition of the eight multiple intelligences. It also provides tips for teachers and parents to help children help themselves. Articles and quizzes can be found to pinpoint which learning style a child favors. Resource links can also be located to help you expand your understanding of multiple intelligences and learning styles of individuals ranging from preschool through high school and beyond.

Westmark School-Learning Styles

http://www.westmark.pvt.k12.ca.us/reading.html

This site provides an overview of the eight multiple intelligences, along with a list of behavior traits accompanying each intelligence. It also includes teaching tips for multiple intelligences through conversations with Howard Gardner. Resource links are provided for learning styles, brain development, assistive technology, and learning differences.

MI—The Theory

http://www.ibiblio.org/edweb/edref.mi.th.html

This site gives a simple, yet informative, explanation of what the traditional intelligence theories are. It introduces Howard Gardner and his ideas on the intelligences. It also includes his most recent research. There are subcategories for each of the intelligences. The site also provides information about how this view has impacted schools historically and how this theory would affect the implementation of traditional education.

The NC Education Place

http://www.geocities.com/~educationplace/

This site reviews the basics of learning styles and gives examples of how to use this information in lesson plans. There are guidelines for a well-rounded classroom and techniques for small groups. There are also links to books and classroom resources. In addition, there is a list of schools in North Carolina that have incorporated these ideas and examples of activities and lessons used. Visitors can also view pictures of the students and teachers from the North Carolina schools.

National Reading Styles Institute (NRSI)

http://www.nrsi.com/

Founded by Marie Carbo in 1984, NRSI is a research-based educational organization dedicated to improving literacy. NRSI offers teachers and parents help in assisting children who display different reading and learning styles: analytical, global, visual, auditory, tactile, and kinesthetic. The site provides parents and teachers with tools to ensure their children's success in reading and learning by contributing reading tips, quizzes, seminars, conferences, book reviews, and opportunities to ask questions.

Multiple Intelligences Developmental Assessment Scale (MIDAS)

http://www.miresearch.org/midas.php

Named after the testing method used to measure multiple intelligence, MIDAS is an organization created to provide others with awareness of the most proficient way of measuring intelligence. The site provides MIDAS reviews and questions based on the theory of Howard Gardner. In addition to offering a MIDAS newsletter, the site recommends material and books, which can be purchased directly through the site, to assist further interest in the mind and intelligence.

Learning Styles and Multiple Intelligence: An Explanation of Learning Styles and Multiple Intelligence (MI)

http://www.ldpride.net/learningstyles.MI.htm

This site provides an explanation of learning styles and multiple intelligence. It describes the six types of learning styles and how each type of learner best retains information. The site also provides viewers with a list of different types of intelligence. It includes a chat room and links to other sites about learning styles and multiple intelligence. There is also information about different learning disabilities.

GT World—Frequently Asked Questions About . . . Testing Our Gifted Children

http://www.gtworld.org/gttest.htm

This website contains the answers to frequently asked questions (FAQs) about gifted children. The FAQ site defines and describes the different types of tests children are required to take during their educational career. The main link for this site is GT World, a publisher of books and articles that are provided as resources for parents. In addition, GT World provides a comprehensive list of web links to reference sites, early entrance college programs, academic programs, mailing lists, and advocacy groups.

Gifted Development Center (GDC)

http://www.gifteddevelopment.com/

This website is a service provided by the Institute for the Study of Advanced Development. The main focus of GDC is to introduce and describe the concept of visual spatial learning. An exercise is provided to discover if someone is a visual spatial learner. In addition, links are provided to other articles and resource materials pertaining to this type of student.

ePALS Classroom Exchange

http://www.epals.com/index.html

While the ePALS website does not provide direct access to lesson plans, teachers are encouraged to learn and share educational experiences and projects through the classroom exchange. This site boasts an e-mail membership of more than 15,000 classrooms in 107 countries. One can search for classrooms in a country and be presented with a short introduction from each participating teacher, who will include information on class size, grade level, and purpose for joining. Dozens of other website resources are also included that will link teachers to recommended educational sites.

Additional Multiple Intelligences Websites

Center for Talented Youth—Johns Hopkins University
http://www.jhu.edu/gifted

Concept to Classroom
http://www.thirteen.org/edonline/concept2class/mi/index.html

The Cook Primary School, Canberra, Australia
http://www.cookps.act.edu.au/mi.htm

DiscoverySchool.com
http://school.discovery.com/lessonplans/programs/
multipleintelligences/

Duke University—Talent Identification Program
http://www.tip.duke.edu

The Gardner School, Vancouver, Washington
http://www.gardnerschool.org/

Harvard Project Zero
http://pzweb.harvard.edu/

Howard Gardner
http://www.howardgardner.com/

Mrs. Young's Page on Multiple Intelligences
http://www.educationalvoyage.com/multiintell.html

National Association for Gifted Children
http://www.nagc.org

The National Research Center on the Gifted and Talented (NRC/GT)
http://www.gifted.uconn.edu/nrcgt.html

New City School, St. Louis, Missouri
http://www.newcityschool.org/

New Horizons for Learning
http://www.newhorizons.org/

Secondary School Educators: Learning Style Assessments Links
http://7-12educators.about.com/cs/learnstyleassess/

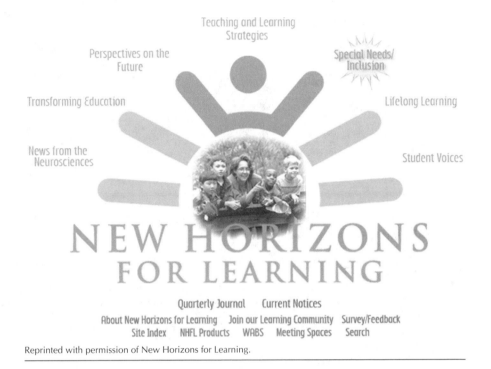

Teaching and Learning
Strategies

Perspectives on the
Future

Special Needs/
Inclusion

Transforming Education

Lifelong Learning

News from the
Neurosciences

Student Voices

NEW HORIZONS
FOR LEARNING

Quarterly Journal   Current Notices

About New Horizons for Learning   Join our Learning Community   Survey/Feedback
Site Index   NHFL Products   WABS   Meeting Spaces   Search

Reprinted with permission of New Horizons for Learning.

ENGLISH FOR SPEAKERS OF OTHER LANGUAGES

It is estimated that by 2020 Hispanics will be the largest ethnic minority group in the United States. For many children, Spanish is the first language learned and continues to be the main language spoken in the home. Additionally, the United States continues to be enriched by immigrants from countries all over the world. Many cities have ethnic enclaves of language minority and immigrant groups. For social studies teachers, it can be a challenge to tailor lessons to meet the needs of students who are English-language learners. The following websites will assist teachers in learning more about the special needs of language minority students and in adapting existing lessons for them.

Bilingual Resources

http://www.eduplace.com/bil/index.html

One of Houghton Mifflin's sites, this is a collection of bibliographies and links to the best and most useful Internet sites for bilingual education teachers. It can be accessed in both Spanish and English.

Welcome-Bienvenidos

Reprinted with permission of Dr. Isabel Schon/California State University.

Barahona Center for the Study of Books in Spanish for Children and Adolescents

http://www.csusm.edu/csb/english/

This site includes a list of recommended books in Spanish, books about Latinos in English, information on workshops and conferences, and hundreds of related links. It can be accessed in both Spanish and English.

Center for Applied Linguistics

http://www.cal.org

Dedicated to "improving communication through better understanding of language and culture," this center's comprehensive site features research, teaching materials, and other resources for ESOL, foreign language, and linguistics.

Dave's ESL Café

http://www.eslcafe.com

This easy-to-navigate site—billed as "The Internet's Meeting Place for ESL/EFL Students and Teachers from Around the World!"—offers many resources for both students and teachers. The "Hint of the Day" and the "Idea Cookbook" offer icebreakers, teaching tips, and games.

ESL Lounge

http://www.esl-lounge.com

This excellent teachers' site is loaded with lesson plans, worksheets, teaching tips, printable board games, and reviews of notable ESL books.

ESL Magazine Online

http://www.eslmag.com

This site features abstracts of articles from the print magazine for English as a second language (ESL) educators. Helpful ESL/EFL links are included.

ESL/Bilingual/Foreign Language Lesson Plans and Resources

http://www.csun.edu/~hcedu013/eslindex.html

Created by a teacher educator at California State University, this site provides many helpful links to lesson plans, resources, study abroad opportunities, and educational standards and frameworks.

Kathy Schrock's Guide for Educators: Foreign Languages, ESL, and General Information

http://discoveryschool.com/schrockguide/world/worldrw.html

Links are included to many sites for foreign-language and bilingual educators. ESL educators will find several online resources that can be used by both teachers and students.

National Association of Bilingual Education

http://www.nabe.org/

This organization is dedicated to promoting equity for language minority students through bilingual education. The site includes the latest updates regarding legislation and policy, articles about bilingual education, conference information, and links to other sites.

National Clearinghouse for English Language Acquisition

http://www.ncela.gwu.edu

This site offers technical assistance on important issues related to linguistically and culturally diverse students. Users will find links to government and professional sites, an online biweekly news bulletin, journal articles and bibliographies, and state laws and associations.

Pizzaz!

http://darkwing.uoregon.edu/~leslieob/pizzaz.html

These creative storytelling activities—both oral and written—can be used with beginner through advanced ESL student levels.

Teachers of English to Speakers of Other Languages, Inc.

Reprinted with permission of TESOL.

TESOL Connects!

http://www.tesol.org

This is the website of Teachers of English to Speakers of Other Languages (TESOL). Users can access news, ESL standards for students pre-K through grade 12, grant information, and a "fax on demand" service to have TESOL documents and applications sent to your fax machine 24 hours a day, 7 days a week.

Website Guides for ESL Students

http://iteslj.org/guides/index.html

Two website guides and accompanying exercises give ESL students opportunities to practice English in relevant, practical ways. Restaurant Row uses hundreds of menus from real restaurants; Internet Movie Database lists more than 180,000 movies.

Additional English for Speakers of Other Languages Websites

Development and Dissemination School Initiative
http://www.alliance.brown.edu/dnd/index.shtml

ESOL Tapestry
http://tapestry.usf.edu/

Ethnologue: Languages of the World
http://www.ethnologue.com/

National Clearinghouse for English Language Acquisition and Language Instruction Educational Programs
http://www.ncela.gwu.edu/about/3_aboutNCELA.htm

SEEDS
http://seeds.coedu.usf.edu/

Transitions Abroad
http://www.transitionsabroad.com/listings/work/esl/bestwebsites.shtml

Virginia Adult Learning Resource Center
http://www.aelweb.vcu.edu/links/esol.shtml

CULTURAL DIFFERENCES AMONG LEARNERS

As the U.S. classroom has become increasingly diverse, educators have responded by trying to incorporate and meet the needs and interests of students who reflect a variety of cultures, religions, and languages. Social studies teachers and students will find the following websites helpful not only for learning more about the beliefs and practices of special populations but also for learning how to structure and monitor learning and classroom exercises to best meet the needs of diverse cognitive styles.

Welcome to Amigos! Bienvenidos a Amigos!

Reprinted with permission of Carmen Guanipa.

Amigos

http://edweb.sdsu.edu/people/cguanipa/amigos

This multicultural site is intended primarily for middle and high school students and their parents and teachers. It includes essays on diversity issues, information on additional resources, personal stories, and intergenerational experiences. The site can be accessed in both Spanish and English.

Awesome Library: Multicultural

http://www.awesomelibrary.org/Classroom/Social_Studies/Multicultural/Multicultural.html

This site provides links and sources for both multicultural and international issues. Users can access information about specific cultural groups and nationalities, retrieve lesson plans, and find pen pals from diverse backgrounds.

Center for Research on Education, Diversity and Excellence

http://www.crede.org

CREDE is a program that seeks to improve the education of students from diverse backgrounds (including culture, language, ethnicity, geographic location, and poverty). The website includes standards, research findings, teaching tools, effective demonstrations, a glossary, and links to hundreds of other sites.

Diversity Dictionary

http://www.inform.umd.edu/EdRes/Topic/Diversity/Reference/divdic.html

Maintained by the University of Maryland, this website offers definitions and brief explanations of words and terms related to diversity issues. Terms are listed alphabetically for easy access. Users can also find links to resources related to specific issues such as gender, ethnicity, religion, and national origin.

Multicultural Pavilion

http://www.edchange.org/multicultural/

This online resource provides reviews, links, and awareness activities for teachers, students, and parents. The Teacher's Corner includes strategies for fostering multicultural understanding in the classroom.

Peace Corps Kids World

http://www.peacecorps.gov/kids

Intended for elementary and middle school students, Kids World provides information about the diverse cultures on earth. The site also stresses the importance of service and volunteerism. Students can apply what they have learned in an interactive game.

Standards: The International Journal of Multicultural Studies

http://www.colorado.edu/journals/standards

This full-text journal includes articles, images, reviews, and links to multicultural educational resources on the Internet.

National Association for Multicultural Education (NAME)

http://www.nameorg.org

NAME is an organization of diverse educators and activists from around the world. This site features publications, position papers, links to related journals and magazines, as well as lesson plans and a reference library.

Valuing Our Differences: Celebrating Diversity

http://www3.kumc.edu/diversity

This University of Kansas website offers a month-by-month calendar replete with multicultural celebrations. Users will find appropriate classroom activities, links to other sites for background information, and references for further reading. Users can also browse by religious holidays, ethnic holidays, and national holidays.

We Hold These Truths to be Self-Evident:
Evidence of Democratic Principles in Our Schools

Part 1: Investigating Special Populations

Gender Issues in Education | Latino Culture | Gay and Lesbian Culture | Issues of Students with Disabilities | African-American Culture | American Indian Culture | Asian American Culture

Reprinted with permission of Carla Mathison.

We Hold These Truths to Be Self-Evident

http://edweb.sdsu.edu/people/cmathison/truths/truths.html

The site guides educators in the exploration of multiculturalism, democratic principles, and special populations in the United States. The Culminating Web Quest Activity can be completed in small groups.

Additional Cultural Differences Among Learners Websites

Center for World Indigenous Studies
http://www.cwis.org/index.htm

Human Diversity Resource Page
http://community-2.webtv.net/SoundBehavior/DIVERSITYFORSOUND

Intercultural E-Mail Classroom Connections
http://www.iecc.org/

The Mid-Atlantic Equity Consortium
http://www.maec.org/

Multicultural Education Through Miniatures
http://www.coedu.usf.edu/culture/List.htm

Multicultural Song Index
http://www.edchange.org/multicultural/arts/songs.html

National Immigration Forum
http://www.immigrationforum.org/

Rethinking Schools
http://www.rethinkingschools.org/

TeachGlobalEd.net
http://www.coe.ohio-state.edu/globaled/home.cfm

INCLUSION OF STUDENTS WITH DISABILITIES

Some 43 million Americans have one or more physical or mental disabilities, and this number is increasing. In 1990, the Americans with Disabilities Act was passed to alleviate the problem of reduced opportunities for individuals with disabilities and the tendency of society to isolate and segregate these individuals. With the enactment of this law, teachers need additional knowledge and skills to assist their students with disabilities.

The Inclusion Network

http://www.inclusion.org/

Sponsored by Cincinnati Bell Telephone and Federated Department Stores, this site serves as a gateway for dozens of resources related to education, employment, community inclusion, and advocacy for people with disabilities.

Council on Exceptional Children

http://www.cec.sped.org/

This huge professional organization is the place to start for information and resources about children and young adults with disabilities. Its site is a gateway to hundreds of useful and practical resources for teachers, administrators, and parents.

Focus on Learning

http://www.focusonlearning.org/learning.htm

This website provides parents and teachers with support, learning resources, and legal information. The Tips for Parents section is equally useful for educators. The Additional Help and Resources section provides links to other organizations that provide assistance.

Additional Inclusion of Students with Disabilities Websites

Center for Applied Special Technology
http://www.cast.org/

Disability Resources, inc.
http://www.disabilityresources.org/INCLUSION.html

Electronic Journal of Inclusive Education
http://www.ed.wright.edu/~prenick/

Florida Inclusion Network
http://www.floridainclusionnetwork.com/

Kathy Schrock's Guide: Special Education
http://school.discovery.com/schrockguide/edspec.html

LD Online
http://www.ldonline.org

Learning Disabilities Resource Community
http://www.ldrc.ca/about.php

Music for Children with Special Needs
http://www.songsforteaching.com/specialneeds.htm

National Association of School Psychologists
http://www.naspcenter.org/inclusion.html

National Association of State Directors of Special Education
http://www.nasdse.org/index.cfm

National Center for Learning Disabilities
http://www.ld.org/

National Dissemination Center for Children with Disabilities
http://www.nichcy.org/

National Inclusive Schools Week
http://www.inclusiveschools.org/default.asp

Northwest Regional Educational Laboratory
http://www.nwrel.org/cfc/newsletters/vol2_is3.asp

PBS Misunderstood Minds
http://www.pbs.org/wgbh/misunderstoodminds/

WORKING WITH AT-RISK STUDENTS

At-risk students present unique problems and often require schoolwide initiatives due to the nature of the socioeconomic causes. The following websites provide research and information on initiatives and strategies that can be used by teachers as individuals or as school leaders.

Pathways to School Improvement

http://www.ncrel.org/sdrs/areas/at0cont.htm

This high-quality site, provided by the North Central Regional Educational Laboratory (NCREL), is an easy-to-navigate point of entry for some of the best resources on the Internet for teaching at-risk students. Be sure to check out the Trip Planner Inventory, a special tool designed to help begin the school improvement process. The Trip Planner helps map out where to go within Pathways to get the information and resources needed to transform local schools.

OVAE At-Risk Youth

http://www.ed.gov/about/offices/list/ovae/pi/hs/atrisk.html

The At-Risk Youth Office supports a range of research and development activities designed to improve the education of students at risk of educational failure because of limited English proficiency, poverty, race, geographic location, or economic disadvantage.

Laboratory for Student Success (LSS)

http://www.temple.edu/LSS/

LSS is a federally funded activity located at the Mid-Atlantic Regional Educational Laboratory at Temple University. It is designed to help schools launch reform initiatives that promote school success for at-risk youth. Its focus is on high academic achievement in urban schools.

National Dropout Prevention Center

http://www.dropoutprevention.org/

This site features research, publications, and information on best practices that are designed to keep kids in school until they earn a high school diploma. This easy-to-use site leads educators to exceptional resources.

Institute for Urban and Minority Education (IUME)

http://iume.tc.columbia.edu/

Dedicated to urban students, their families, and the educators who serve them, this site offers exceptional information about working with at-risk students but also includes resources on many other issues affecting the success of urban youth.

Council of Great City Schools

http://www.cgcs.org

This "organization of the nation's largest urban public school systems, advocating K–12 education in inner-city schools," takes on the most challenging of educational issues in this nation's most daunting settings. Its website provides excellent resources for those who share its mission and goals.

Middle Web

http://www.middleweb.com

A service of the Edna McConnell Clark Foundation, Middle Web is a comprehensive resource for information, news, and tips on best practices to promote success for middle school youngsters from all walks of life. This award-winning site offers stories of real teachers and real schools struggling with the challenge of standards-based reform.

Additional Working with At-Risk Students Websites

Colorado Department of Education (CDE) At-Risk Students/ Prevention Initiatives
http://www.cde.state.co.us/index_atrisk.htm

National Academic Advising Association
http://www.nacada.ksu.edu/AboutNACADA/index.htm

National Association for the Education of Homeless Children and Youth
http://www.naehcy.org/index.html

National Center for Children in Poverty
http://www.nccp.org/index.html

National Clearinghouse on Child Abuse and Neglect Information
http://nccanch.acf.hhs.gov/index.cfm

National Mental Health Association
http://www.nmha.org/index.cfm

Stand Up for Kids
http://www.standupforkids.org/

U.S. Department of Education Office of Safe and Drug-Free Schools
http://www.ed.gov/about/offices/list/osdfs/index.html?src=oc

FAMILY INVOLVEMENT IN EDUCATION

This critical variable in school success can be expanded with help from the information contained on these websites.

Children, Youth and Family Consortium

http://www.cyfc.umn.edu/

The Children, Youth and Family Consortium at the University of Minnesota provides both parents and educators with excellent resources and links that help parents participate meaningfully in the education of their children. This site is particularly well equipped with resources supporting stepfamilies and children of divorce. It also houses parent support groups and links to interactive sites that allow parents to seek advice and counsel from other parents and from youth-serving professionals.

About.com

http://home.about.com/home

About.com is one of the most comprehensive resource sites on the Internet. Use it as a gateway to search for help on virtually any topic. From the Home and Family page, scroll down to the section on parenting. It includes information on school success, parenting strategies for children and adolescents, help for parents of special needs children, advice for single parents and stepparents, and a host of other critical topics for parents and educators. For teachers, this is an excellent place to find information to give to parents who are helping their children overcome specific problems and challenges.

National Parent Information Network

http://www.npin.org

The National Parent Information Network provides a comprehensive library of publications about parenting, parent involvement in school, and successful child-raising practices. Most of the material is in full-text versions and can be downloaded or printed on a home or school computer. The publications on this site cover behavior and discipline, school performance, and coping with high-risk behavior. It is one of the most comprehensive and authoritative resources available for educators and families.

Family Education

http://www.familyeducation.com/home/

FamilyEducation.com is an engaging, interactive information center for parents of K–12 students. It includes articles, tips and advice, discussions, downloads, and a chance to ask the experts for help and support. Confronting challenging topics, this site handles delicate issues with solid advice and dignity.

U.S. Department of Education

http://www.ed.gov/admins/comm/parents/list.jhtml

The U.S. Department of Education provides free, high-quality materials that help promote parents' involvement in their children's education. Some of the most useful publications come from the "Helping Your Child" series—a collection of publications designed to help parents foster healthy development, productive behavior, and success in school. The "Family Involvement in Education" publications focus on building productive collaborations among the school, the home, and the community to improve schools and boost student achievement. Publications devoted to "Learning Activities" and "Reading Improvement" suggest specific ways that parents can help their child extend school learning.

National Parent Teachers Association

http://www.pta.org

The website of the National PTA not only keeps parents up to date on the activities of the association but also provides links to hundreds of child-advocacy groups around the world. If schools are looking for guidance on family-friendly programs and parent involvement, this is the place to begin.

Additional Family Involvement in Education Websites

AARP Grandparent Information Center
http://www.aarp.org/families/grandparents/

America's Promise Alliance
http://www.americaspromise.org/

Colorado Family Literacy Consortium
http://www.coloradoliteracy.net/

Connect for Kids
http://www.connectforkids.org/

Harvard Family Research Project
http://www.gse.harvard.edu/hfrp/index.html

National Center for Family Literacy
http://www.famlit.org/

National Coalition for Parent Involvement in Education
http://www.ncpie.org/

National Urban League
http://www.nul.org/

Parent Advocacy Coalition for Educational Rights
http://www.pacer.org/

Parents for Public Schools
http://www.parents4publicschools.com/

Standards-Based Lesson Planning with the Internet

There are basically two approaches to using the Internet in lesson planning (and hence instruction) to achieve objectives set as a result of the standards-based movement (see next section): **teacher-originated plans**, but with Internet resources infused into the plan, and **Internet lessons plans**, authored by others but modified by you for your students and state standards. The chapters in this book are dedicated to providing you easy access to these resources, and chapter 1 includes the major multidiscipline websites.

TEACHER-ORIGINATED INTERNET-INFUSED LESSON PLANS

This is the traditional approach to lesson planning, in which a teacher has an idea for a lesson plan. However, when using the Internet, teachers *infuse* resources from websites into their lessons. There are three main ways to integrate the Internet resources into the instruction:

1. **Content.** This would take the form of either background information for the teacher, content to integrate into the lesson, or content to use with the students.
2. **Teaching materials.** Teaching materials from maps, primary documents, music, images that can be converted into transparencies, short stories, graphic organizers in Microsoft Word or PDF format, and so on, are available from Internet sites like those found in this book.
3. **Interactive activities.** Simulations, games, puzzles, searches, online tours of historical sites, WebQuests, and so on, can be integrated into the learning experience.

   Finding the best resources requires teachers to carefully consider the sponsor.

CRITERIA FOR SELECTING WEBSITE RESOURCES

A primary consideration is the validity of a website's assets. Some websites are inaccurate, biased, or purposefully misleading. This makes websites different from a textbook or courseware package by a national publisher, professional organization, or the government, which has typically undergone review and editing to ensure accuracy and a balanced presentation.

You can minimize the risks of invalid or inaccurate information or faulty strategies by focusing on websites sponsored by recognized and reputable institutions, such as museums, school districts, universities, libraries, and national organizations for teachers. Extensions identify types of institutions: .com (dot-com) is used for commercial enterprises, and the content of such sites is unregulated. Other specific extensions can be found on the links of educational institutions (.edu), nonprofit organizations (.org), and government websites (.gov).

The following questions are helpful to ask when evaluating a website:

1. Are the goals and motives of the author and sponsor stated and clear?
2. Is the sponsor of the website known and credible?
3. Is the author of the materials on the website credible or an expert?
4. Do the aesthetics, graphics, content details, spelling, grammar, and so on, indicate that the site has been thoughtfully organized and published?
5. Is the site dated?
6. Are the content and materials accurate, up-to-date, and usable?
7. Are the resources grade-appropriate?
8. Is advertising clearly labeled as such?
9. Is there a way for you to respond to the sponsor or author?
10. Can you count on the website to exist in the future?

These are the questions we asked ourselves as we searched the Internet for the resources that would be most helpful to you.

MODIFIED INTERNET LESSON PLANS

The Internet has a large number of lesson plans of varying comprehensiveness, detail, and length. You should review the **multidiscipline websites** in chapter 1 as well as websites cited in chapters 3 through 9. No matter how good a resource may appear, it would be a rare occasion that a teacher could (or should) take a resource off the Internet "shelf" without modifying and improving it for use in her or his classroom and to meet local or state standards.

The modified Internet lesson approach is used when a teacher modifies and adapts a lesson plan found on the Internet to his or her students and circumstances. Internet lesson plans are different from activities and tasks because they tend to be comprehensive (i.e., they include goals or standards, content, a sequence to follow, tasks, materials, etc.) by having links to resources or downloadable attachments like PDF files. For Internet lesson plans selected from either general searches or site-specific searches, there are a number of other indicators of a well-developed plan that you should also consider. And even the best plans should be modified to meet your students' needs and your state's standards.

CRITERIA FOR SELECTING INTERNET LESSON PLANS

The following criteria should be used for selecting Internet lesson plans:

1. **Standards**. Is the plan tied to national or state standards?
2. **Instructional sequence**. Is there a clear and detailed explanation of the sequence of the instruction?
3. **Rigor**. Does the plan challenge students with tasks and activities that require critical thinking and self-discipline?
4. **Creativity**. Does the plan creatively engage students with opportunities to further develop basic skills; a variety of strategies; and meaningful, grade-appropriate content?
5. **Resources**. Are there resources, such as well-crafted handouts or links to other high-quality websites?
6. **Evaluation**. Is there an evaluation component?

The extent to which something on the Internet that is *called* a lesson plan actually *is* a lesson plan—rather than an activity or task—is based largely on how many of these six components are found in the plan. The extent to which it is evaluated as excellent depends on the quality of the components.

The blossoming of the Internet has changed the opportunities to significantly improve the lesson plans we use to teach students. The accountability aspects of the **standards movement** have given even greater impetus to the need to use Internet resources. States that fail to meet expectations can lose federal funding, and schools that fail to meet state expectations can be closed. Teachers are on the front lines and, arguably, feeling more pressure to have their students succeed than at any other time in the history of American education.

NATIONAL STANDARDS

Standards-based education is a relatively new phenomenon in education. It has many goals, not the least of which is to develop more uniform expectations for what is to be learned throughout the United States and to measure in some uniform way the success of each student as he or she progresses through the schools.

Although the standards movement predates President George W. Bush's January 8, 2002, signing into law of the **No Child Left Behind Act of 2001 (NCLB)**, NCLB places the movement in a national context with a national impetus. It redefines the federal role in education and is intended to close the achievement gap between disadvantaged or minority students and their peers in both general and discipline-specific literacy. NCLB, more than any other legislation in American history, moves the United States closer to a national curriculum by mandating that each state establish standards and measure its students' success at meeting those standards. To define those standards, the states have relied on the guidelines in the NCLB (see Figure 12-1) and on professional organizations, such as the NCSS.

Figure 12-1 No Child Left Behind

The following two articles provide an analysis of the NCLB and are available online through the **Education Resource Database** (typically referred to as "ERIC") http://www.eric.ed.gov, a major source of research in education:

- ED477723 *Implications of the No Child Left Behind Act of 2001 for Teacher Education.* ERIC Digest. Trahan, Christopher 2002.
- ED478248 *The Mandate to Help Low-Performing Schools.* ERIC Digest. Lashway, Larry 2003.

Figure 12-2 The Nation's Report Card

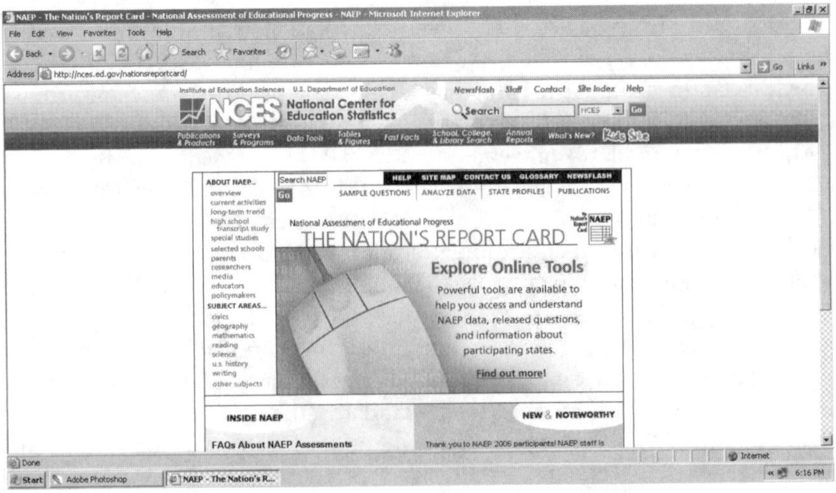

In addition to these analyses, two key sources on how well American students are doing in school are available on the Internet. One, the **Nation's Report Card,** at http://nces.ed.gov/nationsreportcard/ (see Figure 12-2), provides national and comparative assessment data on students' knowledge. The other, the Organization for Economic Co-operation and Development's (OECD) **Programme for International Student Assessment,** at http://www.pisa.oecd.org/knowledge/home/ intro.htm, provides comparative data on high school students' performance from an international perspective.

PROFESSIONAL ORGANIZATIONS' STANDARDS

The movement to establish a more uniform curriculum evidenced in the No Child Left Behind legislation also motivated the professional organizations for each of the teaching fields to develop standards and to provide resources such as lesson plans and materials through the Internet to achieve those standards. To comply with NCLB, most states have adopted and modified the standards recommended by each discipline's professional organization. As a result, the math, reading, and writing skills and the knowledge (content and skills unique to each discipline) of the social studies that you will likely be expected to achieve with your students due to NCLB were most probably defined or heavily influenced by the NCSS and the other social studies related national associations.

STATE STANDARDS

Your state standards can be found at http://edstandards.org/Standards.html#State (Figure 12-3) or http://www.aligntoachieve.org/AchievePhaseII/basic-search.cfm.

Figure 12-3   State Standards Home Page

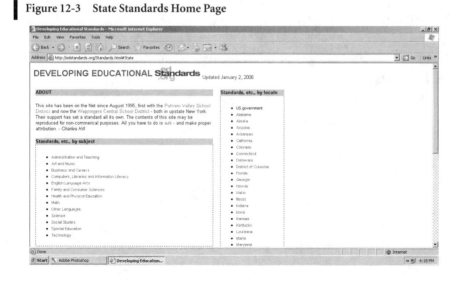

In the final analysis, your state will formulate and set the standards you are expected to achieve in your classroom. Two dominant approaches are used to determine if the standards are being met:

1. **"High-stakes testing"** typically uses a point-in-time approach by using a paper-and-pencil test to determine skills like reading, mathematics, and critical thinking. Which subjects are tested and whether social studies is included are decisions made by each state.

2. **Lesson plans tied to state standards** in specific subject areas require teachers to indicate what specific state standard is being met by the lesson plan. The assumption is that every student will acquire the skill or knowledge prescribed in the standard upon completion of the lesson plan. It is also expected that through these subject-specific lesson plans students should also gain the kinds of general basic skills assessed in high-stakes testing.

CATALOGING INTERNET RESOURCES

The new technology allows you to download lessons, materials, and activities developed by practitioners, publishers, and organizations from across the country to be integrated into your lesson plans for your students. However, one of the new challenges presented by the volume of materials available by way of the Internet is the problem of keeping track of your materials, documents, and websites. By carefully organizing and cataloging your resources, you will be in a much better position to improve the quality of your instruction by being able to conveniently modify and add resources to lesson plans used one year before using the plan again the next year. The following are some ideas on how to manage your newly found resources.

By creating unique folders under "My Documents" on your PC and your "Favorites" folder on your browser, you can create folders for, as an example, history, then a subfolder for U.S. history, and then folders by periods (Federalist, Jacksonian era, etc.). Each of those could be subdivided into the following:

- Background (for background information for the teacher)
- Lesson plans
- Course materials (rubrics, handouts, etc.)

The same idea could be applied to geography, economics, and so on.

Teacher's Tool Kit

Professional growth and development are crucial to a teacher's success. Social studies teachers have a variety of tools on the Internet to enhance their instruction and professional growth. Three of the most useful are professional organizations; electronic journals, newspapers, and news sources; and sites on classroom management.

PROFESSIONAL ORGANIZATIONS

In addition to the National Council for the Social Studies, social studies teachers have a number of professional organizations that provide guidance, support, and materials for the teaching of the content area. In many cases, membership is not even required to access the excellent resources available for educators and students. Some of the best are listed here in alphabetical order.

American Anthropological Association

http://www.aaanet.org

Provides an overview of what anthropology is, free access to several publications, and links to anthropology resources on the Internet.

American Council of Learned Societies (ACLS)

http://www.acls.org

The ACLS is a federation of 61 scholarly organizations related to the social sciences. Education-related projects include a K–12 program designed to improve humanities education in the schools. Also included is information on teacher exchanges with other countries.

American Educational Research Association

http://www.aera.net

This network features online resources, such as educational reports, abstracts, archives for three professional journals, and news and jobs postings. Information about other Internet resources is also provided.

American Forum for Global Education (AFGE)

http://www.globaled.org

The AFGE promotes "the education of our nation's youth for responsible citizenship in an increasingly interconnected and rapidly changing world." The site also allows an exchange of ideas and provides instructional materials and professional development opportunities for teachers and administrators.

American Geographical Society

http://www.amergeog.org

In addition to information about the organization and its membership, this site includes abstracts and images from the *Geographical Review*, geographic photo displays, and 3D virtual tours.

American Historical Association

http://www.theaha.org

Billed as the professional association for all historians, this organization has a K–12 teaching specialization and offers joint membership with other related organizations. Links to other sites are also provided.

American Political Science Association (APSA)

http://www.apsanet.org

The APSA is the world's largest organization for the study of political life. Membership benefits include two quarterly publications, interdisciplinary affiliations, and free electronic notification of research news and Washington, D.C., alerts.

American Psychological Association

http://www.apa.org

The national organization for psychologists and mental health professionals also offers comprehensive information for educators, parents, and teens. Students can access information about career planning, education programs, and college summer programs.

American Psychological Society (APS)

http://www.psychologicalscience.org

The APS's Teaching Resources section offers an excellent overview of the research and application of the field. All major subdisciplines are included, as well as exemplary syllabi and PowerPoint presentations.

American Sociological Association (ASA)

http://www.asanet.org

For high school teachers, this site has several useful features in addition to general membership information. It has a K–12 collaborative program with information on the Advanced Placement Examination, as well as an excellent Teaching Resources Center for high school teachers, which includes syllabi, primers, videos, and other instructional materials. Students can access the ASA Resources for Students section, which discusses honors programs, research support, and careers in sociology.

American Studies Association (ASA)

http://www.georgetown.edu/crossroads/asainfo.html

The ASA promotes the study of past and present American culture. The online newsletter provides full-text curriculum articles for teachers and administrators.

Reprinted with permission of the Association of American Geographers.

Association of American Geographers (AAG)

http://www.aag.org

The AAG is an educational and scientific society that provides publications and resources for the teaching of geography. The site features hands-on learning activities and readings in world and U.S. geography. Links to related organizations and sites provide further resources and materials.

Association for Supervision and Curriculum Development (ASCD)

http://www.ascd.org

The ASCD's emphasis is on K–12 educational leadership and curriculum. The site includes articles and news stories on timely topics, samples from *Educational Leadership*, and information on professional development.

Geographic Education National Implementation Project

http://genip.tamu.edu/right.htm

This consortium on professional geography associations seeks to improve education in the discipline. Links to other organizations and ideas for staff development are included. A biannual newsletter can also be accessed from the site.

Reprinted with permission of Global TeachNet, National Peace Corps Association.

Global TeachNet

http://www.rpcv.org/pages/sitepage.cfm?id=59&category=3

This network, organized by the National Peace Corps Association, seeks to bring global perspectives to U.S. classrooms by disseminating global education materials and resources to K–12 teachers.

National Association of Economic Educators (NAEE)

http://ecedweb.unomaha.edu/naee/naeepamp.htm

The NAEE seeks to encourage and support objective economic education programs at all levels. It serves as a dissemination organ by which ideas, lessons, and effective practices are exchanged among educators.

National Association for Humanities Education (NAHE)

http://www.nahe.org

This professional organization of teachers and scholars in the humanities also includes museum directors and other interested individuals. Links to museums, libraries, and Internet resources are provided, as well as information about the association's journal and newsletter.

National Association for Multicultural Education

http://www.nameorg.org

NAME is composed of a diverse group of educators and activists from around the world. It publishes position papers, a professional journal, and lesson plans all related to issues of diversity.

National Council on Economic Education (NCEE)

http://www.ncee.net

The organization from which to get official standards and guidelines for economic education. The site provides the latest news in the field, online lessons, and links to other helpful sites.

National Council for Geographic Education (NCGE)

http://www.ncge.org

The NCGE offers publications, geography resources, and links to other sites. Information about upcoming activities, annual meetings, and award programs is also provided.

National Council for the Social Studies (NCSS)

http://www.ncss.org

The NCSS is the nation's largest and oldest professional organization devoted to social studies education. On this site, teachers can find national curriculum standards, journals and publications, and teaching resources.

National Education Association (NEA)

http://www.nea.org

The NEA is the nation's largest association of professional educators. Its website has been nationally recognized for being informative and user-friendly. Included in this comprehensive site are the NEA Code of Ethics, school district statistics, links to educational policy sites, online multimedia teaching resources, and many other articles and materials of use to classroom teachers.

National Geographic Society (NGS)

http://www.nationalgeographic.com

The familiar yellow-bordered magazine is just one of the many resources available through the NGS. Of particular interest to educators are the Geography Education, Info Central, and World Magazine for Kids features.

National Middle School Association (NMSA)

http://www.nmsa.org

The NMSA is an organization for middle-school-level educators and administrators. This website offers discussion of timely topics and controversies, K–12 teacher resources, and links to libraries and museums, among other services.

Organization of American Historians

http://www.oah.org

This organization, devoted to the study of American history, offers precollegiate teaching units written by teams of teachers and historians using primary documents. It also offers links to other associations related to history and its teaching.

Phi Delta Kappa (PDK)

http://www.pdkintl.org

PDK is an international organization of professional educators with an emphasis on public schools. This site provides summaries of educational research, information on travel and professional development, and partial access to articles in *Kappan Magazine.*

World History Association (WHA)

http://www.woodrow.org/teachers/world-history

In partnership with the Woodrow Wilson Leadership Program for Teachers, the WHA hosts an annual meeting, publishes conference papers, and provides teaching materials and modules on its website.

ELECTRONIC JOURNALS

Keeping abreast of new teaching techniques and curriculum issues can be a daunting prospect for classroom teachers. Fortunately, the World Wide Web is now home to a variety of professional journals that can keep us informed about current practices and controversies. The following journals permit either full or partial access to contents free of charge. In some cases, a modest subscription fee is required for full access to all features.

American Diplomacy

http://www.unc.edu/depts/diplomat

This electronic journal features free subscription to the quarterly publication. Articles include commentary and analysis on American foreign policy. The archive allows users to access past articles, reviews, and related websites.

American Quarterly

http://crossroads.georgetown.edu/aq/alphsub.html

American Quarterly is an interdisciplinary journal for the study and teaching of American culture. Nonmembers can access full-text articles by browsing the site's archive.

Anthropology and Education Quarterly

http://www.aaanet.org/cae/aeq/index.htm

This journal publishes scholarship on schooling in social and cultural contexts, on human learning both inside and outside of schools, and on the teaching of anthropology. The website provides a table of contents and abstracts of current and past issues.

APA Monitor

http://www.apa.org/monitor

Full-text access to the American Psychological Association's online newsletter. The Education feature includes articles for psychology teachers of all levels, as well as model school programs and fairs.

Bryn Mawr Classical Review and the Medieval Review

http://ccat.sas.upenn.edu/bmcr/subform.html

Free subscription to two electronic journals published by Bryn Mawr College. The first features reviews of current scholarly works in the field of classical studies. The second offers reviews of current work in all areas of medieval studies. Both have searchable archives.

CSS Journal

http://www.webcom.com/journal

Computers in the Social Studies focuses on promoting computers and related technology in social studies classrooms at all education levels. In addition to provocative articles, the site has a searchable archive, provides links to other social studies sites, and has sample historical documents.

Reprinted with permission of Earthworks.

Earthworks

http://www.utexas.edu/depts/grg/eworks/eworks.html

This refereed journal focusing on contemporary geographic issues offers full access to its contents. The Web in Education feature is especially useful for teachers.

Education Week

http://www.edweek.org

Online newspaper for educators that includes news items, commentaries, and special reports. A searchable archive and States Pages make this site useful for retrieving specific information quickly. The enormously helpful *Teacher Magazine* can also be accessed from here.

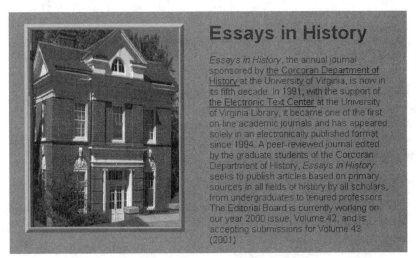

Essays in History

Essays in History, the annual journal sponsored by the Corcoran Department of History at the University of Virginia, is now in its fifth decade. In 1991, with the support of the Electronic Text Center at the University of Virginia Library, it became one of the first on-line academic journals and has appeared solely in an electronically published format since 1994. A peer-reviewed journal edited by the graduate students of the Corcoran Department of History, *Essays in History* seeks to publish articles based on primary sources in all fields of history by all scholars, from undergraduates to tenured professors. The Editorial Board is currently working on our year 2000 issue, Volume 42, and is accepting submissions for Volume 43 (2001).

Reprinted with permission of Essays in History, a journal of Corcoran Department of History at UVA.

Essays in History

http://etext.virginia.edu/journals/EH

An annual publication by graduate history students at the University of Virginia, this electronic journal offers full-text articles that span all fields of history. Past issues (starting with 1990) are also available.

Foreign Affairs Magazine

http://www.foreignaffairs.org

The Weekly Column features excellent analyses of international developments. Related websites include links to world news, commentary, multicultural resources, and regional studies.

Internet Archaeology

http://intarch.york.ac.uk

Registration to access the full text of articles is required, but free. Teachers of anthropology and history will benefit from the scholarly articles and discussions.

Journal of Economic Education

http://www.indiana.edu/~econed/index.html

Content and pedagogy are both addressed in this electronic journal, which features innovative articles on a variety of cutting-edge teaching media.

National Review Online

http://www.nationalreview.com

Although only partial contents are available on this site, it is nonetheless a useful resource for obtaining conservative perspectives on political issues. "Websclusives" offers several features available only on the website.

Perspectives Online

http://www.theaha.org/perspectives

The electronic newsletter of the American Historical Association features full access to scholarly articles on historical topics, as well as innovative strategies for teaching history.

Phi Delta Kappan (PDK)

http://www.pdkintl.org/kappan/kappan.htm

Full-text articles are available on a variety of education-related topics. The results of the annual PDK/Gallup Poll of the public's attitudes toward the public schools can be found here.

Political Science Quarterly

http://www.psqonline.org

This electronic journal offers a partial sampling of full-text articles and reviews. Civics and government teachers can read insightful analyses of current political issues and events.

Progressive Review

http://www.princeton.edu/~progrev/prog.html

This electronic magazine, "dedicated to social justice," offers full-text articles. Published monthly during the school year.

PS Online

http://www.apsanet.org/PS

PS Online is the American Political Science Association's online version of *Political Science and Politics*. The teaching feature includes guidelines for K–12 teachers of civics and government, as well as a forum to exchange teaching ideas with colleagues.

Scholastic

http://teacher.scholastic.com/index.htm

The online version of the popular school magazine offers a number of classroom-tested resources, ideas, and reproducibles. Students will enjoy completing the online social studies activities and tours.

Teacher Magazine

http://www.teachermagazine.org

Includes discussion of contemporary educational issues, practical teaching advice and solutions, recommended books for teachers and students, summaries of research, and commentaries on a wide variety of topics.

Teaching Sociology

http://www.lemoyne.edu/ts/tsmain.html

Although a subscription is necessary to fully access articles, the table of contents for each issue is provided on the website, making it a useful tool to find specific articles.

Reprinted with permission of Yale Political Quarterly.

Yale Political Quarterly

http://www.yale.edu/ypq

Published by Yale undergraduates, this site has several useful features for educators: full-text articles, a compilation of political quotes, political links, and access to back issues.

ELECTRONIC NEWSPAPERS AND NEWS SOURCES

The hallmark of the social studies has always been staying abreast of current events. The Internet, with its immediate coverage of worldwide events and issues, is a powerful resource for teachers and students. Several newspapers, magazines, and news services allow us to obtain up-to-the-minute information, analyses, and visuals of breaking stories. Many sites also offer entertaining news quizzes to test understanding.

American Journalism Review Newslink

http://ajr.newslink.org

Offers thousands of links to newspapers, magazines, and news services worldwide. Also includes articles on journalism.

Ultimate Collection of News Links

http://pppp.net/links/news/report.html

More than 10,000 links to newspapers and magazines from around the world are provided on this site.

The New York Times Learning Network

http://www.nytimes.com/learning

In addition to providing up-to-the-minute information on current events, the Learning Network links users to additional news and education resources on the World Wide Web. Its strength lies in the considerable archives of its host, the *New York Times*. Teachers will find the daily lesson plans—with thematic connections across the curriculum—very useful. Students will like the interactive news quizzes and the opportunity to send questions to *Times* reporters.

News Directory

http://www.ecola.com/news/press

This comprehensive site provides links to hundreds of daily and nondaily newspapers in the United States and worldwide. Other news sources included are magazines and television.

Awesome Library: Reference and Periodicals

http://www.awesomelibrary.org

The Reference and Periodicals feature on this site allows users to search for news and current events by Subjects, Cities, Countries, USA, and World. By selecting Current Events, visitors are taken to a gateway page that includes lessons, online news sources for all grade levels, and virtual field trips.

Time for Kids

http://www.timeforkids.com

An online version of the print magazine. Elementary students can select from the "grades 2–3" and "grades 4–6" renditions. The site contains current events in both text and multimedia formats. Users can also research past events via a searchable archive.

CNN Interactive

http://www.cnn.com

The cable network's home page includes up-to-the-minute news coverage on a variety of topics. Because it is based on the television show, nearly all the stories are accompanied by an image or map. Users can also listen to stories in RealAudio, view video clips, and search the archives.

Reprinted with permission of KidNews.

KidNews

http://www.kidnews.com

Linking students and teachers from around the world, this site encourages students to write and submit news stories on a variety of topics. Teachers can also use the Adults Talk feature to exchange teaching ideas and lesson plans.

Newsday Project

http://www.gsn.org/project/newsday

Students not only can learn about national and international news and issues on this site but also can create their own newspapers. Opportunities exist for students to gather and write news stories, edit articles, create layouts and graphics, and publish the finished product. A link on the site, *Middlezine*, is an electronic magazine created by eighth graders covering an array of topics such as literature, art, sports, and science.

I'm a Kid

http://www.weeklyreader.com

Coverage of current events can be accessed on a number of grade levels: pre-K, 1, 2, 3, 4, 5, 6, and teen. Options for teachers and parents are also available.

Current Events in the Social Studies Classroom

http://www.eduplace.com/ss/current/index.html

Monthly highlight of an issue in the news. Each discussion ends with thought-provoking questions suitable for classroom use. The entertaining Current Events Challenge is divided into Grades 1–3, Grades 4 and Up, and For Teachers.

Learning Resources

http://literacynet.org/cnnsf

Using interactive learning activities, this site seeks to improve literacy and understanding of current events by providing news stories that are easier to understand than standard newspaper articles. In addition to reading the text, students can listen to and/or view a video clip. The Instructor Page offers teachers lesson plans and ideas for individualized learning.

Nettizen

http://www.nettizen.com/newspaper/

Online newspaper directory, organized by region and featuring headlines and articles from around the world. Photos, maps, and political cartoons can also be accessed.

Online NewsHour

http://www.pbs.org/newshour

The website of the popular television news show with Jim Lehrer offers transcripts of current broadcasts (some segments are available in RealAudio).

Also included are background briefings, a discussion forum, and an archive, among other features. Of particular note for students is the News for Students section.

U.S. Newspaper Links

http://www.usnpl.com/

This website provides links to newspapers and TV stations throughout the United States.

CLASSROOM MANAGEMENT

Very few professions ask 22-year-olds to manage 150 people a day and oversee the successful completion of a task. Managing the classroom is one of the most daunting issues for many new teachers. Without classroom management, social studies cannot be taught. Even experienced teachers find significant new challenges that test their ability to manage students and the learning process. The following sites offer some ideas on classroom management strategies.

Works4Me

http://www.nea.org/helpfrom/growing/works4me/library.html

This NEA site offers suggestions on classroom management, as well as school climate and instructional planning. New and experienced teachers will find more than 400 "tips" organized around categories such as Getting Organized, Teaching Techniques, and Using Technology. Users can link to searchable libraries, forums, and resource units.

You Can Handle Them All

http://www.disciplinehelp.com

The website offers background information on psychological dispositions associated with misbehavior. Broken down into Misbehaviors at School and Misbehaviors at Home, this is a very useful tool for diagnosing and finding solutions for 117 common misbehaviors.

The Really Best List of Classroom Management Resources

http://drwilliampmartin.tripod.com/reallybest.htm

Hundreds of clickable links to experienced teachers' insights, advice, and dozens of links to other resources on classroom management.

Discipline by Design: The Honor Level System

http://www.honorlevel.com/HLS_INTRO.HTML

This site offers a description of the Honor Level System, a proactive approach to dealing with student discipline. Originally developed at the middle school level, it is now used at all grade levels in many U.S. schools. Eleven discipline techniques are highlighted and juxtaposed with classroom management strategies that backfire.

Dr. Mac's Amazing Behavior Management Advice Site

http://maxweber.hunter.cuny.edu/pub/eres/EDSPC715_MCINTYRE/715HomePage.html

This CUNY professor's website offers thousands of tips on managing student behavior and creating a positive classroom environment. It provides detailed directions for implementing useful interventions.

Teacher Vision

http://www.teachervision.fen.com/page/5776.html?detoured=1

On this web page from Teacher Vision, experienced teachers offer behavior management tips and classroom organization strategies that have worked for them.

ERIC Online Documents

http://searcheric.org/

ERIC has two extensive documents on classroom management. *Positive Classroom Management: A Step-by-Step Guide* (ED433334) is a 134-page guide to classroom management. *The First Six Weeks of School* (ED442770) provides information on practices as well as activities to ensure the first 6 weeks get off to a good start.

REPRODUCIBLES, GAMES, AND PUZZLES

ABC Teach

http://abcteach.com/

More than 5,000 printables are included on this website. The worksheets are arranged by topics such as flash cards, theme units, clip art, and fun activities.

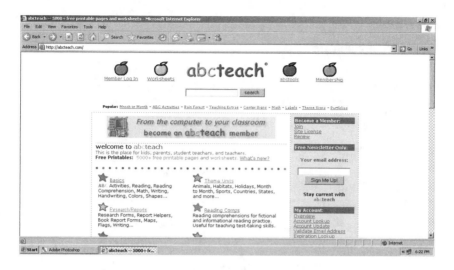

Education Express

http://www.schoolexpress.com/fwsindex.php

This site has close to 10,000 worksheets that are downloadable and categorized by teaching fields. Primarily intended for elementary level.

PBS TeacherSource: Social Studies

http://www.pbs.org/teachersource/soc_stud.htm

Users can search this site by grade level and topic. In addition to lessons and activities, recommended books and links are also provided.

Region 15 Graphic Organizers

http://www.region15.org/curriculum/graphicorg.html

This Connecticut school district offers a well-organized listing of graphic organizers that are available in both English and Spanish.

Teacher Vision Printable Graphic Organizers

http://www.teachervision.fen.com/page/6293.html?detoured=1&for printing=1

Dozens of downloadable and printable graphic organizers for use primarily in the elementary school classroom. Note that membership is required for some items.

KidsCom

http://www.kidscom.com

This site for kids offers games, chat rooms, webtoons, and a "Create" page that allows students to create cards, scrapbooks, stories, and original music.

Puzzle Maker

http://www.puzzlemaker.com

Users can create and save puzzles online using teacher-supplied words, pregenerated vocabulary lists, and clip art. Some of the puzzle types include word search, cryptograms, crossword, and math squares.

Additional Teacher's Tool Kit Websites

American Memory: Places in the News
http://memory.loc.gov/ammem/gmdhtml/plnews.html

BBC News
http://news.bbc.co.uk

Children's Express
http://www.childrens-express.org

Kathy Schrock's Guide for Educators: News Sources and Newspapers
http://discoveryschool.com/schrockguide/news/nsp.html

The New York Times on the Web
http://www.nytimes.com

Oneworld.net
http://www.oneworld.org/themes/country/front.shtml

Online Newspapers
http://www.onlinenewspapers.com

Time.com
http://cgi.pathfinder.com/time

Topics Online
http://www.topicsmag.com